L.L.Bean®
Fly-Tying Handbook

OTHER L.L. BEAN HANDBOOKS

L.L. Bean Fly Fishing Handbook

L.L. Bean Fly Fishing for Bass Handbook

L.L. Bean Fly Fishing for Striped Bass Handbook

L.L.Bean®
Fly-Tying Handbook

DICK TALLEUR

LYONS PRESS

Printed in Canada

10 9 8 7 6 5 4 3 2 1

Design by Desktop Miracles, Inc., Dallas, TX

Library of Congress Cataloging-in-Publication Data

Talleur, Richard W.
    L.L. Bean fly-tying handbook / Dick Talleur.
        p.   cm.
    Includes index.
    ISBN 1-55821-708-8
    1. Fly tying—Handbooks, manuals, etc.   I. L.L. Bean, Inc.   II. Title.   III. Title: L.L. Bean
beginner's fly-tying handbook.   IV. Title: Beginner's fly-tying handbook.
SH451.T288   1998
632'.952—DC21   98-6125
                                                                                                          CIP

CONTENTS

1

Getting Started

FLY TYING IS REALLY NOT VERY DIFFICULT, but it can seem that way to the beginner. It was considerably harder for those of us who began many years ago, because we didn't have the learning aids that are available today. Not that many people tied flies back then, either, and few of those who did were willing to share.

I saw a fly tied for the first time when I showed up for my first lesson. It was a Mickey Finn streamer, a pattern that's included in this book. I managed to struggle through a couple of them, with my instructor coaching me through each step. Things would have gone much better if I'd had a bit of orientation first. I would suggest this to all beginners. If you can watch someone with adequate basic skills tie a few flies, your fledgling attempts will be much easier.

While I've tried to be as explicit and detailed as possible in this book, both in text and photographs, no book is quite as helpful as a good teacher. You *can* learn to tie flies by following the instructions in these chapters, but you'll progress more easily and quickly with a tutor at hand, and the book serving as a text.

As your tying skills and interests develop, you will need and want some additional tools and instruments. I'll describe many of these in the rest of this chapter. In the beginning, however, a few basic tools will suffice. They are:

1. Fly-tying vise.
2. Fly-tying scissors.
3. Bobbin.
4. Hackle pliers.
5. Bodkin or dubbing needle.

The Vise

The fly-tying vise is a specialized instrument of which there are a number of types. The most common, and the one I recommend for beginners, is the simple **lever/cam** design. The jaws, or chuck, of the vise are tightened around the hook by pushing down a lever at the rear. The spread of the jaws is easily adjusted to accommodate hooks of larger and smaller wire diameters, or thicknesses.

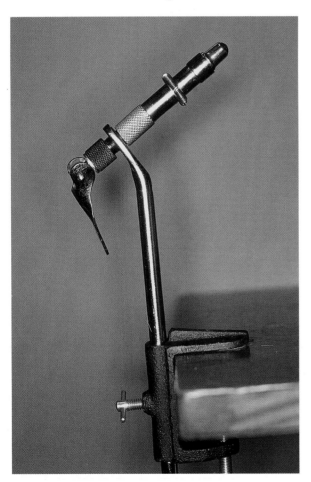

A typical Thompson A-type fly-tying vise.

Most lever/cam vises are in proper adjustment for the hook at hand when the lever is at approximately the 5:30 position. However, each has its own idiosyncrasies. If your vise comes with an instruction sheet that provides information about this adjustment and other important details, please refer to it before you insert your first hook. Lacking this, follow the six o'clock rule, and play with the adjustment until the hook is held firmly. BUT (and this is a big but) don't force the jaws to close by exerting extreme pressure.

There are lots of really heavy-wire hooks out there, and eventually you may encounter them. Atlantic and Pacific salmon flies often use such hooks, as do many saltwater patterns. It's important to avoid trying to mount a hook into the jaws of your vise that's heavier—meaning thicker—than the vise was designed for. If you can't close the jaws with ease when they are at their maximum width adjustment, don't force it, as damage will almost surely result.

There are two schools of thought on how a hook should be mounted in a vise. One school advocates burying the barb and point, thus avoiding having your tying thread get cut by the point. The other school advocates gripping the hook by the lower part of its bend and allowing the barb and point to be exposed, which optimizes access to the hook from the rear. I use both methods, depending on the type and size of hook. This will be explained in the forthcoming pages.

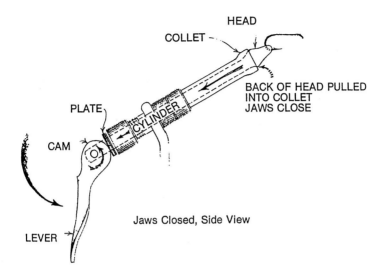

A functional drawing of the vise.

In the more costly types of vises, other features are incorporated. One that can be quite helpful is angle adjustment, which enables you to make the attitude of the collet tube that holds the jaws either steeper or flatter. This attitude is also related to hook size and type. For example, it's much easier to work on smaller hooks with the collet tube at a steep angle.

Another useful feature is the ability to revolve, or rotate, the jaws—and concurrently, of course, the hook. This works best with vises that have the angle-adjustment feature, so that the tube and jaws can be set at level, allowing you to look at and work on both sides of the fly. This is not the same as a full-rotating vise, which is a more sophisticated instrument that uses a special design to enhance rotating capability.

Vises come with either a **C-clamp** or **pedestal** mounting arrangement. The clamp offers the advantage of adjustable height and is considerably lighter in weight—an asset when traveling. The pedestal offers the flexibility of being able to work on any flat surface without regard to thickness or overhang. Also, it does not interfere with a lap drawer, such as might be found in a typical fly-tying desk.

Keeping your vise at the proper height is an important factor in your tying efficiency and comfort. There being no way to change the height of a pedestal vise, you may have to put something under its base if it needs to be raised, or heighten your chair seat if the vise needs to be relatively lower. Some kind of office chair that is height adjustable is ideal; however, such a major purchase is usually not necessary, because vises today are designed with the typical tying setup in mind.

Scissors

If you have only one pair of scissors, they should be fine enough for close work. This means that the tips should come to a sharp point and be precisely matched. There's a liability, however, to such scissors—the cutting of heavy or tough materials. At the very least, you must avoid cutting such materials with the tips of the scissors; instead work well down into the blades. Better to have a second, sturdier pair at hand. They need not be expensive. Nail clippers are useful for cutting thick quills, oval tinsel, plastic wraps, and similar materials.

There is a wide variety of scissors on the market. In addition to the sharpness and fineness factors, there's the matter of fit. This applies to the size of the finger loops and to the overall length of the scissors. Many tyers, myself included, keep their scissors in their right hand at all times, with the fourth finger through one of the loops. In order for you to do this without getting stabbed, the scissors must be long enough to extend beyond the palm of your hand. For those with small hands, 3½ inches (90 mm) may suffice. I find that 4 inches (100 mm) works better.

The size of the finger loops is also a matter of personal fit. Some people like oversize finger loops. I like a closer fit, as I feel it gives me more precise control. Try several, and see what feels good.

Bobbin

The fly-tying bobbin is a most useful tool: It replaces several tedious operations formerly done by hand, eliminates a lot of knot tying, and maintains tension on the thread. Far and away the most important consideration with a bobbin is that the tip of the tube be perfectly smooth; otherwise, it will cut the thread, which is a nightmare. Certain bobbins have been known to develop sharp-edged tubes over time simply through wear—that is, the action of the thread. Some bobbin manufacturers have switched to ceramic tubes or inserts to prevent this.

If you find yourself constantly breaking thread when you're using only moderate tension, or if you notice thread fraying all the time, suspect your bobbin. Try to

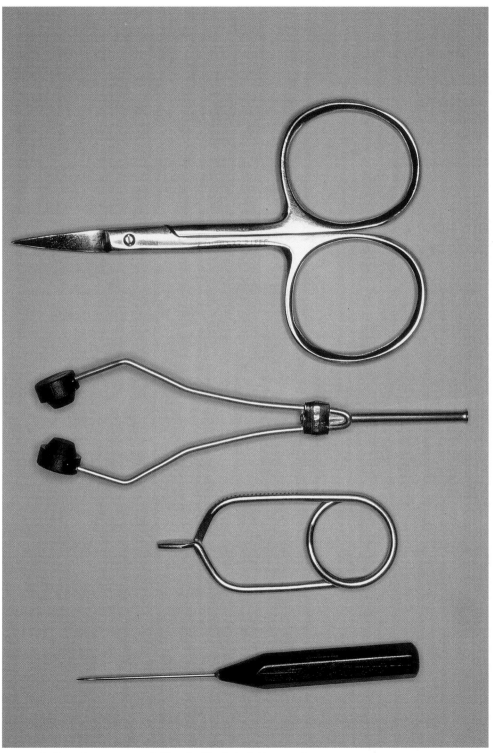

Basic tools. From the top: scissors, bobbin, hackle pliers, dubbing needle.

borrow one that's known to be nonlethal; get an experienced tyer to help, if possible. You may find that it's not you, it's your tool—in which case you return it, of course.

Most bobbins need to be adjusted for proper tension. The idea is that the bobbin should hang in suspension without feeding out thread by virtue of its own weight. The thread should feed out readily and smoothly, but under a modicum of tension. This is achieved by mounting a spool of thread in the tool and adjusting, or bending, the limbs of the wishbone until you like the feel.

Bobbin Threader

This tool is truly a "one-trick pony," so to speak. It's used to draw the tying thread through the tube of the bobbin. Generally, it consists of a sharply pointed loop of fine wire. Lacking this, you can get by with a piece of fairly stiff monofilament, doubled over. The dental floss threaders that are sold in drugstores make great bobbin threaders.

Hackle Pliers

Hackle pliers are also a special-purpose instrument. Their main purpose is to grip a feather while you wrap it to form a hackle. There are a number of designs on the market today, some of which are quite a departure from the basic or conventional. While I'm very much in favor of innovation, I believe that it must stop short of gimmickry. Therefore, I strongly advocate simple hackle pliers that embody these features: a firm yet gentle grip, a comfortable size and shape for handling, and a sufficient weight to hold a feather in position when hanging suspended. The latter is important because quills have a certain stiffness and will try to unwrap themselves unless tension is maintained.

After thirty-five years of tying, I still prefer what are called English hackle pliers, which meet these criteria. The grip can be improved by adding a small piece of heat-shrink tubing to one of the jaws; this also lessens the possibility of breaking feathers. A word of caution: Don't get one of those miniature pliers that look so cute in the store. These are harder to handle and lack sufficient weight. Small flies can be worked on just as easily with normal-sized pliers; it's the jaws that count, not the overall size of the tool.

Some people use those little spring-loaded electronics clips as hackle pliers. I don't approve of them for general work, as they are too light and the wrong shape.

However, they are very useful for certain operations. One of these is the twisting and wrapping of peacock herl, which we'll be doing later in the book. They don't cost much, and are very handy.

Hackle Gauge

In dry-fly tying, the proper sizing of hackle is very important. Eventually, you'll be able to flex a feather, look at the barb length, and tell what size it is. In the beginning, though, you may need the assistance of a hackle gauge. I would suggest a model that has a small peg, pin, or something around which you can bend the feather to simulate its being wrapped around the hook. There are several that can be attached to the post of the vise—a most convenient feature.

Bodkin

Also called a **dubbing needle,** this tool is simply a sharp-pointed instrument that is used for such tasks as picking out fur bodies and applying head cement. My favorite bodkin is a hardware store item called a pin vise. It enables you to change points anytime you choose. What more need be said?

There's another method for picking out and fuzzing up fly bodies, using a little piece of "male" Velcro—that is, the side with the tiny hooks. It works great and never cuts the thread.

Hair Evener

This device is also called a **stacker.** Its function is to enable you to quickly and effectively align the tips of bundles of hair that are to be used in making wings and such. Here again, a number of designs are available. The most important consideration is that the tool be of adequate size; those with narrow tubes will only work with small bunches of hair and are quite ineffective for evening up bundles of calf tail hair, which is crinkly and requires a generously sized tube. Remember, you can operate on smaller bunches with a wide-tubed stacker, but not vice versa.

Hair Packer

This is a very specialized instrument that is used when spinning deer or similar hair. As the bunches are tied in place, the packer is used to compress the hairs, which improves the results. It's a low-cost item in fly shops. You can also make a serviceable one yourself by disassembling a typical ballpoint pen and using the housing.

Whip Finisher

The most effective knot for tying off the thread after you complete a fly is the whip finish. It is sometimes used during intermediate steps as well. It is easily done by hand, but even more easily and quickly done with a good tool. I particularly like the Matarelli whip finisher. Here again, it's advisable to buy the larger model, which is much more versatile.

Half-Hitch Tool

In the next chapter, you'll learn the basic knots. While I can assure you that making half hitches by hand is very simple, you should be aware that there is a tool for doing it. Unless you're one of those people who just love tools, I see no need for this one.

Materials Clip

This is an adjunct to the vise that holds onto certain types of materials while you perform subsequent operations. The best example is securing ribbing tinsel while tying the body of a fly. Many vises come equipped with a materials clip. In any case, it's a useful and low-cost add-on.

There are other devices that serve specialized purposes in fly tying. You'll undoubtedly find out about them as you go along, and it's your decision as to which, if any, will be helpful. As I stated earlier, I'm all for innovation, but only in the interest of progress. Essentially, my rule is not to use a tool for any task that I can do just as well by hand.

Chemistry

Fly tying has it own chemicals—substances that are used to finish off heads, protect vulnerable components, and enhance certain materials. Perhaps the first question that needs to be addressed is: Why use a head finish in the first place? The answer may seem obvious—but not so fast. Actually, I believe that, given modern synthetic waxed threads and well-tied whip-finish knots, fly heads could be left unfinished with minimal danger of their coming apart. After all, how long does the average fly last, anyway?

But then, with unfinished heads, you have to be careful not to damage the thread with forceps or some other tool when you unhook fish. Also, flies simply don't look as pretty without a nicely finished head. So I vote for lacquer or cement of some type. In fact, I use two coats on larger flies with more prominent heads.

There are quite a few **head cements** and **lacquers** available today. In most cases, they use a solvent of some type. These include acetone, methyl ethyl ketone (MEK), toluol, and lacquer thinner. Pretty potent stuff. Usually, the stores carry the thinners, so that you can buy the right one for whatever lacquer or cement you prefer, in modest quantities. This is important. While a general lacquer thinner may seem to work on a particular product, it may actually be changing the formula. So while some coatings may respond well to a general-purpose thinner, it's best to use the one that's recommended.

Most head finishes are of the hard variety. However, there are a few that are described as "flexible." These are clear compounds that dry to a tough, rubbery finish, rather than a hard, brittle one. They have adhesive qualities and are useful in keeping stuff together. They can also be used to perform repair jobs, such as mending splits in jungle cock feathers.

It may be that a common clear head lacquer is all you will ever require. However, many tyers find other substances to be of considerable value. Among these are the so-called "superglues" of the cyanoacrylate type. They are extremely strong and fast drying and can be used to protect quill bodies and other delicate components. At this writing, Zap-A-Gap seems to be the most popular.

Epoxy is sometimes used to finish off heads on larger flies, especially those with eyes on them. Certainly, there is nothing stronger or more durable. The process is a bit tedious, however, what with the mixing and drying time. Even the five-minute variety requires a number of hours before the fly can go fishing. The main thing is to get the mix right, because if the proportions aren't very close to being exactly equal, it will never thoroughly cure. If that should happen, try to remove the first coat with a little acetone and stir up a new batch. Also keep in mind that epoxy won't set up properly in an overly cold environment.

When you buy epoxy, make sure it's the clear type. Either the regular or the five-minute will work; the only problem with the latter is that it doesn't allow you much working time. I suggest that you avoid those two-part finishes intended for coating rod wrappings, if you want a thick, protective head; they are very low in viscosity.

There's a little problem with applying epoxy over waxed thread, because it doesn't penetrate the way solvent-based thinners do. For security's sake, you might first apply a coat of well-thinned clear lacquer and allow it to dry completely.

We are now seeing products that are described as being, shall we say, "environmentally considerate and responsible." Most recently, we've begun to see lacquers with water-based finishes. They are truly solvent-free and can be thinned and cleaned up with plain water. They come in various colors, and there are two types of clear: hard and flexible. (More about these in chapter 8.)

Threads

There is an amazing variety of threads on the market today. It makes sense to use the type and size (thickness) of thread that's best suited to the task at hand. However, this doesn't mean that larger flies are always best tied with heavier threads. It's a matter of function and style.

Generally speaking, finer threads work better than thicker ones. You get better gripping power with more wraps of fine thread than you do with fewer wraps of thick thread, and a much neater effect to boot. This is especially true when finishing off heads. I do most of my tying with 8/0 Uni-Thread, except where extra-strength hook coverage is required.

There's the question of plain versus waxed thread. Back when silk was the only game in town, proper waxing was a necessity, for several good reasons. With synthetics, most of these reasons have disappeared. However, a little wax can still be helpful when you're working with certain types of materials.

One consideration with waxed threads is the penetration and adhesion of head finishes. With solvent-based lacquers, this problem is minimized, as the solvent abets penetration and bonding. With epoxy and the new water-based finishes, there can be a problem. For this reason, I do one of two things when using these latter finishes: Either I avoid using waxed thread, or I apply a coat of solvent-based lacquer before I apply the final finish coat.

2

The Basics

PRACTICALLY ALL OPERATIONS IN FLY TYING involve thread. Thus, you need to know how to load the thread into the bobbin, attach it to the hook, wrap it around the hook, and, later, secure and detach it. This requires mastering one simple wrapping technique and two basic knots: the half hitch and the whip finish. In fact, if you are reasonably competent with the whip finish, you may never want to resort to the half hitch.

Loading and Tying on Thread

First, let's load the thread into the bobbin. You might want to refer to the comments on bobbin adjustment in chapter 1. If you are satisfied that your bobbin is properly adjusted, proceed as follows:

1. Seat the spool in the bobbin.
2. Run out 6 to 7 inches (150 to 175 mm) of thread.
3. Run the bobbin threader of your choice through the tube and out the other end.
4. Run the thread through the loop of the threader and pull it through the tube.

No problem with this, right? Check to see that the thread feeds smoothly. If further bobbin adjustment is needed, do so at this time.

Now you're ready to tie the thread onto the hook. This is simply a matter of wrapping the thread over itself along the hook shank. First, be aware that the thread—and, in fact, almost everything in fly tying—is wrapped over and away from the tyer. In other words, if you were looking at the process from the eye end of the hook, the wraps would be going clockwise.

I realize that a certain percentage of the world's population is left handed. No problem; it's absolutely okay to face the vise the other way and do things as nature programmed you. The rules and instructions still apply; just reverse the right-hand-left-hand commands.

Here's the procedure for tying on:

1. Hold the bobbin in your right hand and the end of the tying thread with your left hand.
2. Position the thread against the far side of the hook.
3. While maintaining tension, wrap the thread around the hook five or six times, working rearward, so the wraps cross over themselves.
4. Release the bobbin and let it hang. Hold the tag end (the excess) of the thread tight with your left hand, applying tension, and trim it off flush with the hook, using your scissors as a lance. This is better than cutting the thread in the normal manner, because no little stub is left.

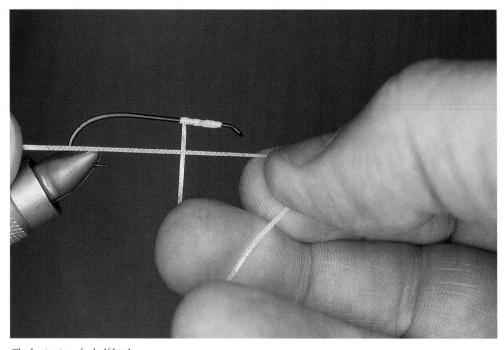

The beginning of a half hitch.

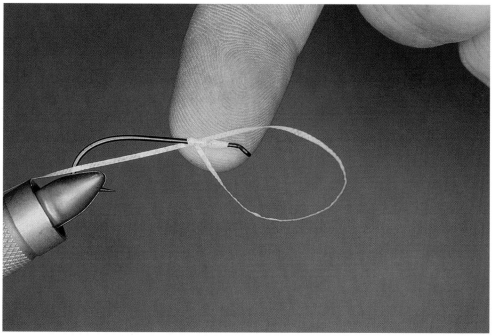

To complete the half hitch, pass the thread loop over the eye of the hook, anchor it against the backside of the hook with a finger, and tighten, nooselike.

As I mentioned, there are only a couple of knots that have application in fly tying: the half hitch and the whip finish. The **half-hitch knot,** or usually a series of several of them, is used to secure a tying operation at some point in the construction of a fly. It is sometimes used by beginners in lieu of the whip finish to tie off at the completion of a fly, but the whip finish is a much more secure knot and should be mastered. Here's how the half hitch goes:

1. With your right hand, twist the thread to form a triangular loop, with the thread crossing in front of itself, and the bobbin off to the rear.
2. Pass the thread around the front of the hook in such a manner that the eye protrudes through the triangular loop.
3. With a finger of your left hand, press the thread against the back of the hook, to keep it from coming undone.
4. Pull the thread from the rear to tighten the loop.

The **whip finish** can be done with one or two hands. The single-handed method is a bit tricky, so I'll teach you the two-handed one here.

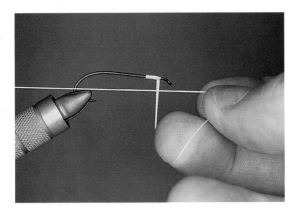

The whip finish begins the same as the half hitch.

Important! As a beginner, you'll be breaking or accidentally cutting the tying thread now and then. In fact, this will happen occasionally even after you've become a master tyer. It's very important to know what to do when this happens. I call this Disaster-Avoidance Technique Number One.

Always have your hackle pliers at hand. If you should break or cut the thread, immediately seize the tag end that's hanging from the hook and maintain tension. Then attach your hackle pliers to it, and let them hang. Now simply tie on again, bind down the hanging tag, release the hackle pliers, trim off both the old and new tag ends, and go about your business.

1. Pull out enough thread so that the bobbin may be laid aside—it is not, and should not be, involved in this procedure.
2. Make a triangular loop as you would with the half hitch, but somewhat larger.
3. With your left hand, hold under tension the side of the loop that passes around the hook, while the other side of the loop—the thread coming from the bobbin—hangs straight out in front of the hook eye.
4. Wrap the thread that you've been holding in your left hand around the front of the hook, passing it back and forth between your two hands as you go. What you are doing is binding the other thread to the hook in nooselike fashion. Make five or six wraps.
5. With your right hand, insert something like a dubbing needle or toothpick into the loop and use it to maintain tension, while holding the other end of the thread with your left hand.
6. Tighten by pulling with your left hand. As the loop becomes tight behind the eye of the hook, withdraw the needle or toothpick and tighten securely.
7. Using your scissors like a lance, cut off the thread.

Before you tie an actual fly, I suggest that you practice these procedures until you are comfortable with them. Once you can execute them with a reasonable degree of skill, you're ready for your first adventure in fly tying.

Hooks and Possible Substitutions

It is my unpleasant duty to inform you that there is virtually no standardization in hook descriptions. You will see specifications such as **4X long, 3X fine, model perfect bend,** and so forth. They are quite arbitrary, and the various manufacturers take considerable liberties in the application of them. Thus, hooks listed as having, for example, a 3X-long shank or 3X-fine wire may differ remarkably

COMMUNITY LIBRARY
Twin Lakes

Borrowed on 10/08/2014 12:37 Till

1) L.L. Bean fly-tying handbook
   Due date: 11/05/2014
   No.: 332100612594
2) Unbroken : a World War II story of survival,
   resilience, and redemption
   Due date: 11/05/2014
   No.: 332101868872

Total on loan : 16

Contact us at 262-877-4281
10/08/2014 - 12:37

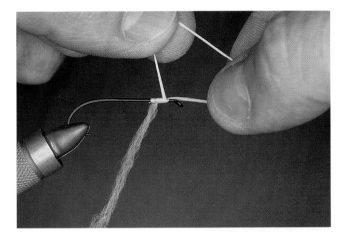

The part of the thread that's coming off the hook is wrapped around the hook five or six times. The part of the thread that goes back to the bobbin forms a standing loop in front. Using both hands, pass the thread under and around the hook, binding the thread that goes back to the bobbin to the hook shank.

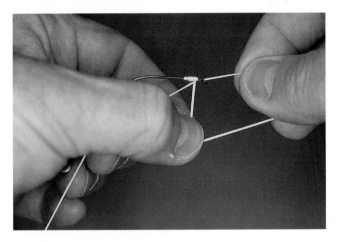

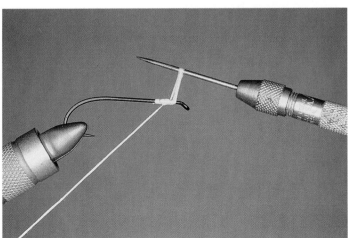

The whip finish is completed by pulling on the thread from the bobbin end, tightening nooselike. Apply tension with a needle or something similar, as shown.

between manufacturers. You can expect to find variations in shank length, wire weight, shape of bend, and other criteria. This can result in variations (usually small) in the tying process and in the appearance and proportions of the finished fly.

Even though it constitutes an imperfect system for describing the characteristics of hooks, you'll be encountering such nomenclature frequently, so let's see what it all means. The term *X* means "extra." Thus, if you see a hook designated as being a size 12, 2X long (2XL), it means that its shank is two hook sizes longer than that of a standard-shanked size 12; in other words, it has the gap (*gape* is the old British term) of a 12 and the shank of an 8.

Since the X system deals in relatives, there must be a benchmark, or starting point. It is generally accepted that a standard-length shank is two times the gap of the hook. As I mentioned, there are variations between manufacturers, but they are usually modest enough not to be a source of trouble. The hooks are sufficiently interchangeable that the same proportions will result in the finished fly.

This is not always the case with wire diameter, which is also defined using the X system. For example, **3X-fine wire** is meant to describe a very fine-wire dry-fly hook. However, the variation between manufacturers is greater in this application, and there doesn't seem to be an agreed-upon benchmark. For example, some years ago, one hook maker put out a dry-fly hook designated 4X fine. It didn't seem all that fine to me. After the judicious application of a micrometer to this hook and another from a different company marked 1X fine, I found the 4X hook to be a hair thicker of shank than the 1X, which is considered standard dry-fly wire. Such discrepancies exist in wet-fly and streamer hooks as well.

The best that I can suggest is that you learn about the various hooks and apply that knowledge to the selection of them. This is of particular importance with dry-fly hooks, where relatively small differences can be meaningful. You might try interrogating the personnel of the store you frequent, to see if they are aware of the idiosyncrasies of the hooks they carry. But don't be shocked if they are not.

As you progress in fly tying, you'll learn more about hooks through your personal experiences and observations. I'm not going to belabor the matter here, but I do think that you should be generally acquainted with hook nomenclature and the fact that it's not entirely accurate. There may well come a time when you'll want to carefully examine the hooks you intend to purchase to be sure they will enable you to successfully tie the shape, style, and weight of fly that you want.

At the risk of dating this book, I provide herewith a listing of the more popular hooks used in fly tying today. It is not a complete listing. New hooks come onto the market fairly frequently these days, and it's really difficult to stay current. However, I think this list provides some valuable orientation. Note that some hooks are listed in two categories; that's because they are in-betweeners.

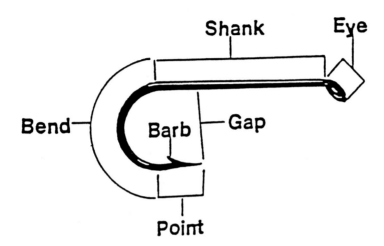

The parts of a hook.

Typical Wet Fly	Daiichi #1550; Mustad #3906; Partridge #G3A; Tiemco #3769[1]
1XL Wet Fly/Nymph	Daiichi #1560; Mustad #3906B or #7957B; Tiemco #3761
2XL Nymph	Daiichi #1710; Mustad #9671; Partridge #D4A; Tiemco #5262
3XL Nymph	Daiichi #1720; Mustad #9672; Partridge #H1A or #D3ST; Tiemco #5263
4XL Nymph/Streamer	Daiichi #1750; Mustad #79580; Partridge #CS17; Tiemco #300
Streamer	Daiichi #2340 or #2370; Mustad #9575 or #3665A; Partridge #CS17; Tiemco #300
Standard Dry Fly	Daiichi #1180 or #1100; Mustad #94840; Partridge #E1A or #L3A; Tiemco #100 or #5210[2]
Long Dry Fly	Daiichi #1280; Mustad #94831; Partridge #H1A[3]

---

[1]Tiemco #3769 has slightly heavier wire.

[2]While all of these hooks are suitable for tying dry flies, there are slight variations in wire diameter, shape, size, and design.

[3]These hooks are represented as being adaptable for tying longer dry flies, such as hopper and stonefly patterns. However, wire thicknesses vary a little, the Mustad being the finest in diameter at this writing.

Some final thoughts on hooks. Today, we return our gamefish to the water, hopefully unharmed. Debarbing the hook is an important part of this process. However, I do believe there are a few exceptions.

Some of today's fly-tying hooks have very small barbs and can be used as is. I don't like to debarb my salmon hooks, because landing an Atlantic salmon, especially a sizable one, is a rare experience and usually a difficult one. Thus, I use hooks with very conservatively sized barbs, such as the Daiichi #2421 and #2441. I feel that with due care and hooks of this type, I can release my salmon with assurance of survival.

It's always best to debarb a hook before tying a fly on it, for the simple reason that the hook might break during the debarbing process. Small pliers or forceps with smooth jaws work fine. Larger, stronger hooks can be debarbed by using the jaws of the tying vise—carefully, of course. I don't suggest this for fine-wire dry-fly hooks; they should be handled more gently.

The idea is to flatten out the barb or cause it to break off. Some hooks, dry-fly models in particular, use a more brittle type of steel, and the barb will usually break off under moderate pressure, leaving a small bump in its place. You'll feel it happen. Don't try to flatten this bump any further; you've done enough.

The Woolly Worm

I CAN THINK OF NO BETTER TYPE OF FLY FOR A STARTER than the Woolly Worm. It is very easy to tie, yet it's very effective on trout, panfish, and even the occasional bass. It can be tied in practically any size and color combination, and it requires very inexpensive materials.

You'll recall that I mentioned in chapter 1 that the hook can be mounted either with the point exposed or with it hidden in the vise jaws. Since we're using a fairly large, strong hook here, I recommend burying the hook point in the jaws. This will effectively prevent you from accidentally catching the thread on the point and cutting it.

With this type of fly, a long feather is required. I advocate tying it in by the tip end, so that its barbs are progressively a little longer as the feather is wrapped forward. This results in a good-looking tapered effect and, I firmly believe, enhances the effectiveness of the fly.

In this lesson, you'll learn three very important techniques, specifically:

1. The thread pinch wrap, which is probably the most important technique in fly tying.
2. Wrapping a hackle that is tied in by the tip.
3. Tying off materials.

You'll also learn about **chenille,** a most user-friendly tying material. This stuff looks like a caterpillar, and well it should, because its name is derived from the French word for that insect.

WOOLLY WORM DRESSING

HOOK:	Medium shank length, 2X to 4X long, fairly heavy wire; see the hook chart in chapter 2 (page 17). Usually tied in sizes 4 to 10.
THREAD:	Black 6/0 or 8/0.
HACKLE:	Black, long, and fairly soft.
BODY:	Medium-thickness black chenille.

I should mention that the proportions of materials are relative to the size of the hook. For larger or smaller hooks, you should use thicker or narrower chenille and larger and smaller feathers, respectively, in order to maintain proportions.

TYING STEPS

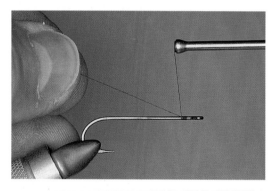

Tying on (step 1).

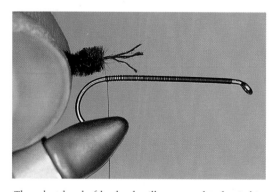

Thread at bend of hook, chenille prepared to be tied in (steps 1-2).

1. Tie the thread on up front just to the rear of the hook eye, trim off the tag end of the thread, and wrap to the rear of the hook, where the bend begins.
2. Cut off a piece of chenille about 5 inches (125 mm) in length. With your thumbnail, scrape off a little of the fuzz at one end, exposing a bit of the thread core.
3. With your left thumb and forefinger, hold the chenille on top of the hook in the position shown.
4. Bring the thread up between your left thumb and forefinger. Pinch together the thread, the exposed core of the chenille, and the hook itself.
5. While maintaining the pinch, sneak the thread downward between your fingers on the far side of the hook, catching the chenille core against the hook shank.
6. Repeat this move several times. Then release the pinch, trim off any excess core material, and take a few firm thread wraps, moving forward by about the thickness of the chenille.
7. Select a hackle feather and prepare it by carefully stripping off the fluffy material around the butt end. Starting at the butt end,

gently stroke the fibers, which are called **barbs,** so that they stick out at approximately a right angle to the quill. Don't break off or cut off the quill, as you'll need this for a "handle" when you wrap the hackle.

8. Near the tip end, stroke back the barbs on both sides, thus exposing the quill. Hold the feather against the bottom of the hook with the good, or shiny, side facing you, and bind the quill to the hook at this spot. The idea is that during wrapping, the shiny side is facing forward.

9. Secure the tie-in by binding down the tip of the feather as you work forward with the thread. Cut off any excess well before you get to the eye area. The thread should now be positioned a little way behind the eye. Leave yourself some space there for tying down the chenille, which is a bit more bulky than most materials.

10. Pick up the chenille and begin wrapping it around the hook. Remember: Always wrap away from yourself. Take one turn behind the tie-in point of the feather, then come in front of it and continue. This protects the quill from the rear, and better positions the feather for wrapping.

11. When you reach the spot where the thread is hanging, proceed as follows: Hold the chenille with your right hand, maintaining tension. Pick up the bobbin with your left hand and lift it over the chenille and the

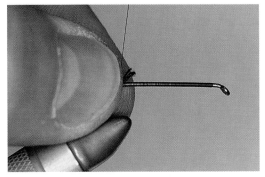

Tying on the chenille with a pinch wrap (steps 3-5)

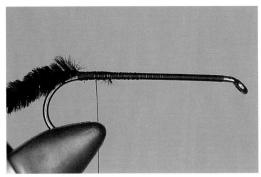

Chenille tied in, thread positioned for tying in the hackle feather (step 6).

A typical Woolly Worm hackle feather, prepared to be tied in (step 7).

The hackle feather tied in, thread wrapped to front (steps 8-9).

Wrapping the chenille (step 10).

The chenille body completed (step 11).

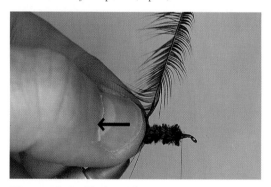

Wrapping the hackle (step 12).

The completed Woolly Worm (steps 13-14).

hook several times. Then transfer the bobbin to your right hand and take several more firm wraps. When you're sure the chenille is securely tied down, cut off the excess and bury the end with a few more wraps. Don't crowd the eye!

12. Pick up the hackle and begin to wrap it, shiny-side forward, in spiral fashion, following the wraps of chenille. Ideally, the quill should sink between the wraps of chenille. Also, it is most helpful to stroke back the barbs with your left hand as you wrap. This helps keep them from getting tangled with the quill, results in a more attractive hackle, and streamlines the shape of the fly overall.

13. This step is optional but, in my opinion, desirable. When you've reached the front of the chenille body, providing you have enough feather left, take two or three additional wraps of hackle, one against the other, stroking back the barbs as you wrap. This puts a good-looking finish at the front of the fly.

14. The hackle feather is tied off in the same manner as was the chenille. Hold the end of the quill with your right hand and perform several or more "lift-over" bobbin moves under firm tension. Transfer the bobbin to your right hand and take a few more firm wraps. When you're sure you've secured the feather, cut off the excess and bind down the stub of the butt.

Now you're ready to execute the whip finish, per the instructions in chapter 2. Afterward, apply at least one coat of head lacquer, allowing for thorough drying between coats.

A little hint: If you plan on tying several Woolly Worms at one sitting, you can conserve on chenille by cutting pieces that are long enough for three or four flies. This reduces the loss that would accrue from waste tag ends with each fly.

Now you've tied your first fly. Admire it, cherish it, fish with it, and save it. I sorely wish that I'd saved my beginning flies, as they would make great keepsakes today, almost forty years later.

It is very common in fly tying and fishing to embellish simple flies with little additions, in the interests of diversity and enhanced attractiveness. We hope, of course, that the fish see it this way. Frequently, a small tag of yarn is added to the Woolly Worm. It could be red, hot orange, bright green, or whatever. The tag is tied in place before the tying of the fly. Here's how it's done:

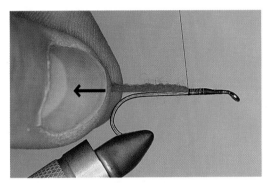

1. Tie on up front and wrap the thread about 25 percent of the shank length to the rear.
2. Cut a piece of yarn perhaps 1½ inches (40 mm) in length. Tie it in with pinch wraps on top of the hook. Trim off the excess.
3. Take hold of the tag with your left hand and apply tension. Then wrap the thread to the rear, binding down the yarn as you go. It is helpful to hold the yarn slightly toward yourself, in order to counteract the torque effect of the thread.

Adding a yarn tag to a Woolly Worm (steps 1-4).

4. When you reach the bend, stop, and trim the tag to the desired length. I would suggest that it be rather short, as shown.
5. Proceed with the Woolly Worm.

Adding a yarn tag to a Woolly Worm (steps 1-4).

Some Woolly Worm Patterns

1. GRIZZLY/BLACK

TAG: (optional) Red or green yarn.
BODY: Black chenille.
HACKLE: Long, soft grizzly (barred rock) rooster feather.

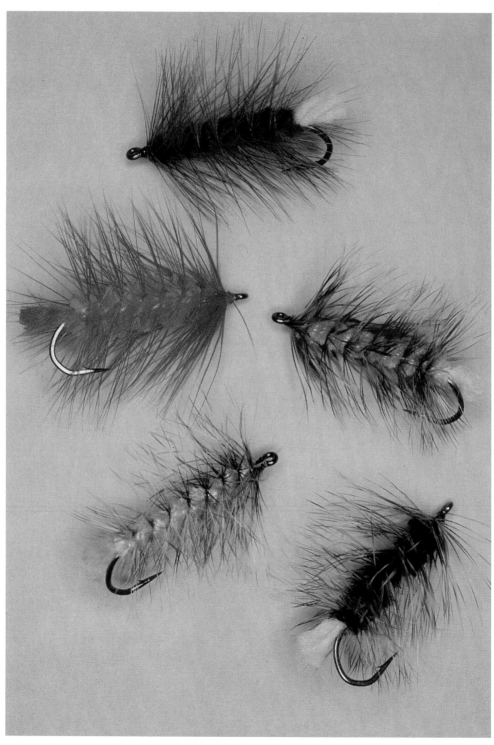

A group of Woolly Worms. Clockwise from the top: Brown/Brown, Grizzly/Green, Grizzly/Black, Grizzly/Yellow, Hot Orange/Hot Orange.

2. GRIZZLY/GREEN

TAG: (optional) Chartreuse yarn.
BODY: Bright green chenille.
HACKLE: Long, soft grizzly rooster feather.

3. GRIZZLY/YELLOW

TAG: (optional) Yellow yarn.
BODY: Yellow chenille.
HACKLE: Long, soft grizzly rooster feather.

4. BROWN/BROWN

TAG: (optional) Red or green yarn.
BODY: Brown chenille.
HACKLE: Long, soft brown rooster feather.

5. HOT ORANGE/HOT ORANGE

TAG: (optional) Orange yarn.
BODY: Orange chenille.
HACKLE: Long, soft orange-dyed rooster feather.

Note: The hooks for these flies are the same as for the one in the tying lesson. If you wish to vary the thread color to better match and complement the colors of the flies, feel free to do so.

4

The Woolly Bugger

L ET'S BUILD ON WHAT WAS LEARNED IN THE WOOLLY WORM LESSON by tying its successor, the Woolly Bugger. Essentially, this is nothing more than a Woolly Worm with a tail. The tail is usually made out of a material called **marabou,** which is a fancy name for turkey body feathers, dyed whatever color. Soft fur from the arctic fox also makes a great tail.

Two new techniques will be demonstrated:

1. Tailing the Woolly Bugger.
2. Weighting a fly.

As with the Woolly Worm, the proportions of materials should be matched up with the size of hook you're using. For this type of fly, I like a hook 3X or 4X in shank length. The size might range from 1/0 to 10. Here, I'm using a size 6.

WOOLLY BUGGER DRESSING

HOOK:	Medium shank length (3XL to 4XL), typically sizes 2 to 10.
THREAD:	Black 6/0 or 8/0.
TAIL:	Black marabou feather.
UNDERBODY:	Soft wire, fine to medium thickness.
HACKLE:	Barred rock (grizzly), long and fairly soft.
BODY:	Medium-thickness olive chenille.

TYING STEPS

Turkey marabou plume before and after center quill is snipped out (step 2).

Turkey marabou plume before and after center quill is snipped out (step 2).

1. As was done with the Woolly Worm, tie on up front just to the rear of the hook eye, trim off the tag end of the thread, and wrap to the rear of the hook. Then create a smooth thread base right ahead of where the bend begins to slope off. Just a couple of layers is sufficient.

2. Select a marabou plume that has soft, fairly straight barbs. If you see that the quill extends out into the part you'll use for the tail, go in with the very tips of your scissors and snip it out below the tie-in point, keeping in mind that the tail will be about the same length as the hook shank. Then strip off the very fuzzy material around the butt end. Be careful, however, not to discard too much material.

3. Stroke the fibers toward the tips with your left hand, bringing them together and neatening them. It is helpful to slightly moisten the feather while performing this operation.

4. Measure the marabou plume against the hook shank. As stated, they should be of equal length. Then set the feather atop the hook and tie it on with a few pinch wraps. Secure it with a series of firm wraps in that area; then trim off the excess as closely as you can.

5. Cut off a piece of wire about 6 inches (150 mm) in length. Remember the little hint at the end of the last chapter about conserving

Tying in and trimming the marabou (steps 3-4).

materials when tying several flies at a sitting? It applies here to both the wire and the chenille.

6. Note that the thread is not involved in affixing the wire; it simply molds itself to the hook as it is wrapped. Abut the wire against the chopped-off tail butts, thus effecting a smooth transition. Wrap it neatly forward, with the turns abutting one another. Stop well short of the eye. You should allow for one full turn of chenille ahead of the wire. Trim off the excess at both ends.

7. This is optional, but important. Spread a coating of adhesive, such as head lacquer or, better yet, Zap-A-Gap, over the top of the wire, and allow it to penetrate between the wraps. This helps secure the underbody.

8. The remaining steps are exactly the same as for the Woolly Worm. Cut off a piece of chenille about 5 inches (125 mm) in length. With your thumbnail, scrape off a little of the fuzz at one end, exposing a bit of the thread core.

9. Tie in the chenille with pinch wraps, secure it, and trim off the tag of the core.

10. Select a hackle feather and prepare it by carefully stripping off the fluffy material around the butt end and stroking the barbs to a right angle to the quill, per steps 2 and

Tying in and trimming the marabou (steps 3-4).

Wrapping on the wire (steps 5-7).

Chenille and hackle feather tied in (steps 8-10).

The completed Woolly Bugger (steps 11-12).

3. Tie it in by the tip end with the good, or shiny, side facing you, secure, and trim.

11. Wrap the chenille, taking the last turn just ahead of the wire. Tie it off, secure it, and trim off the excess.

12. Wrap the feather as instructed for the Woolly Worm—shiny-side forward, in spiral fashion, following the wraps of chenille, stroking back the barbs as you go. At the front, take two or three additional wraps of hackle, one against the other, stroking back the barbs as you wrap. This puts a good-looking finish at the front of the fly. Tie off as previously instructed, do a whip finish, apply lacquer, and head for the water.

Woolly Buggers are tied in many different color combinations. My all-around favorite is the same as the one we just tied, except with a peacock herl body.

Another popular embellishment to this fly is a bit of glitz in the tail. This could take the form of a few strands of Krystal Flash, Glimmer, Flashabou, or any of such shiny materials. Just don't overdo it; too much flash has an adverse effect on fish.

Some Woolly Bugger Patterns

1. Black/Grizzly/Peacock

TAIL: Black turkey or fur marabou.
BODY: Peacock herl.
HACKLE: Long, soft grizzly rooster feather.

2. Pale Olive/Brown/Pale Olive

TAIL: Pale olive turkey or fur marabou.
BODY: Pale olive chenille.
HACKLE: Long, soft brown rooster feather.

3. Pink/White/Pink

TAIL: Pink turkey or fur marabou.
BODY: Pink chenille.
HACKLE: Long, soft white rooster feather.

A flock of Woolly Buggers. From the top: Purple Flasher, Brown/Olive, Black Psychedelic, Hot Pink/White, Black/Grizzly/Peacock.

4. Purple Flasher

TAIL,
BODY, &
HACKLE: All purple; materials as per usual.
FLASH: Purple Krystal Flash or similar; a few strands mixed into the tail.

5. Black Psychedelic

TAIL: Black turkey or fur marabou.
BODY: Iridescent dubbing: a mix of rainbow Lite Brite and black fur.
HACKLE: Long, soft black rooster feather.

Note: The hooks for these flies are the same as for the one in the tying lesson. If you wish to vary the thread color to better match and complement the colors of the flies, feel free to do so. A weighted underbody is generally used on Woolly Buggers.

5

The Soft-Hackle
Wet Fly

THE SO-CALLED SOFT-HACKLE WET FLY HAS BEEN with us for centuries. The oldest of the British angling books describe patterns that are, in essence, soft-hackles. They would surely work just fine today in their original dressings.

This type of fly is suggestive, in a general but apparently convincing manner, of emerging insect life. It serves as a very good imitation of emerging caddisflies as they transform from what is known as the pupal to the adult stage. Soft-hackles are also suggestive of emerging mayflies, small crustaceans, and other forms of aquatic life.

The list of dressings for soft-hackles is practically endless. Entire books have been written about them, and many magazine articles. To my way of thinking, the patterns that will become your favorites are those that work where you fish. Thus, it's helpful to learn as much as possible about the insects in your fishing area.

In this lesson, we'll tie a peacock-bodied soft-hackle and add a bit of **tinsel** for a highlight. This is not the same as Christmas tree tinsel; it's made especially for fly tying. There are several types, the most common being flat and oval; we'll use the latter here. The two most popular colors are gold and silver. With today's flat tinsel, which is usually made of Mylar, you'll find gold on one side and silver on the other. Both types come in several widths or thicknesses. Here, we'll use fairly fine oval.

Peacock herl is a wonderful material that appears in so many of our historic "killer" flies. It can be purchased either in bundles or by the tail. For most applications, the bundled stuff works just fine. However, if you get into streamer tying, in which peacock fronds are frequently used in a different manner, you'd be better advised to buy the tails.

The techniques we'll examine in this chapter are:

1. The peacock herl body.
2. The oval tinsel rib.
3. The soft-hackle collar.

PEACOCK SOFT-HACKLE DRESSING	
HOOK:	Wet fly, regular shank length, typically sizes 8 to 16. Refer to the hook chart in chapter 2 (page 17).
THREAD:	Black 6/0 or 8/0.
RIBBING:	Oval gold tinsel.
BODY:	Peacock herl.
HACKLE:	Grizzly (barred rock) hen feather.

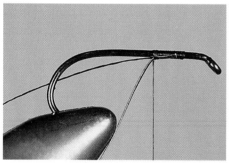

Tying in the tinsel. Note that the thread tag is not trimmed off (steps 1-2).

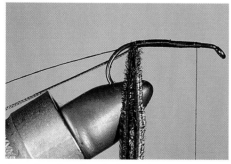

Peacock tied in, thread advanced to the front (steps 3-4).

In chapter 1 you'll recall that I mentioned the spring-loaded electronics clip as being very helpful in working with peacock herl. The reason is that peacock herl quills are often quite flat and resist being twisted together with thread, which is necessary for reasons of durability. The electronics clip is the ideal tool for gripping and twisting them. I think this more than justifies the couple of bucks it costs.

TYING STEPS

1. Tie on near the front of the hook, leaving a fairly long tag of thread—about 5 inches (125 mm)—which is not to be cut off, as you will use it subsequently.
2. Cut a piece of tinsel a few inches in length and tie it in on the bottom of the hook. Then hold both the tinsel and the thread tag with your left hand and, while applying tension, bind them down along the bottom of the hook shank, stopping at the bend. This is similar to the procedure described in chapter 3 for adding a yarn tag to a Woolly Worm (see page 22).
3. Select a few pieces of peacock—let's use five here—and cut back the tips a little, in order to do away with the most brittle part. Tie them in as a bunch by the trimmed tip ends at the rear of the hook, where the bend begins to slope off. Then wrap the thread forward to where you'll want the body to end, leaving plenty of space for tying off the peacock and

the tinsel, wrapping the hackle, and doing the whip finish.

The reason for tying in the peacock herl by the tips is twofold: to reduce bulk and to maximize herl. The quills are much thicker at the butt ends, and the herl more sparse.

4. Be sure that both the peacock and the thread that was left hanging are located together at the bend of the hook and that there is no space between the two; otherwise, the thread will come across the peacock and may cut it. Pick up the tag end of thread and start twisting it together with the peacock, in effect forming a virtual chenille. Don't take too many twists at first, because the thread might sever the herl.

Note: If by some chance you've forgotten and have cut off the thread tag, no sweat. You can either tie in another piece of thread or form a long loop and cut off one side of it, whichever you find more convenient.

5. Begin wrapping the herl and thread "chenille" around the hook, working forward with each wrap abutting the one before it. Continue twisting the thread and herl as you go. If you run into difficulty with twisting, you can resort to the electronics clip or regular hackle pliers.

6. When you reach the spot where the thread or bobbin was left hanging, tie off and trim the peacock as you would chenille.

7. Pick up the tinsel and spiral-wrap it forward over the herl. Here, you have the option of reverse-wrapping, as I'm doing here, so as to further reinforce the peacock. This simply involves wrapping toward yourself instead of away. You'll get four or five turns. Try to keep them as evenly spaced as possible. Secure and trim the tinsel tag end.

8. The soft hackle is done in a somewhat similar manner as the large hackles of the Woollies, with a couple of departures. Select a hackle feather whose barbs will extend about 1½ times the gap of the hook, give or take a little.

Wrapping the peacock and thread combination (step 5).

The peacock body completed (step 6).

Reverse-wrapping the tinsel ribbing (step 7).

The completed ribbing (step 7).

The hackle feather tied in place (step 8).

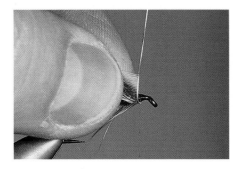

Stroking back the barbs while wrapping (step 9).

Prepare it by carefully stripping off the fluffy material around the butt end and stroking the barbs to a right angle to the quill, per previous instructions. Tie it in by the tip end with the good, or shiny, side facing you, secure, and trim.

9. For working with this smaller feather, I'd suggest using your hackle pliers. Wrap the feather as instructed for the front end of the Woollies, shiny-side forward, stroking back the barbs as you go, so that the hackle forms a graceful cornucopia around the fly body. Two wraps should be sufficient—at the very most, three. You don't want to overdress your soft-hackle wets. In some cases, one turn is all you'll want.

10. Whip-finish, lacquer the head, and you're done.

The completed fly (step 10).

If you wish, you can perform an operation known as **folding the feather** ahead of time. This makes forming the cornucopia somewhat easier. Here's the drill:

1. After preparing the feather, take hold of it by the butt end with your hackle pliers.
2. Grip the pliers with the fourth and fifth fingers of your right hand, leaving your thumb and forefinger free for action.
3. Hold the tip of the feather with your left hand. With the quill under tension, use your right thumb and forefinger to stroke the barbs to whichever side of the quill they naturally belong. The feather is now ready to be tied in and wrapped.

I urge you to master this technique, because it's used in several important fly-tying operations. We'll revisit it several times throughout the book.

I might mention that many soft-hackle dressings call for bodies made of a stranded material called **floss**. Again, this is fly-tying floss, not the stuff your dentist yells at you for not using properly. It comes in many colors and a variety of thicknesses. A thin

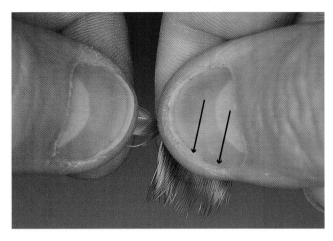

How to fold a feather and gather barbs (supplemental steps 1-3).

skein of floss is preferable for the relatively small hook sizes usually used for these flies. Tyers of Atlantic salmon flies use floss a great deal. A few of them even insist on floss made of silk, which was and is the traditional raw material.

The Bead-Head Enhancement

A fairly recent addition to the fly tyer's arsenal is the introduction of beads with holes drilled through them. The addition of these beads to standard patterns has imbued these flies with a remarkably different sort of action or behavior in the water, more like a miniature jig. They also, of course, add weight.

At this writing, beads are available in several metallic colors, including silver, gold, brass, and black, and also in a range of sizes. Glass beads are available as well; I haven't tried them yet. Typically, the beads are drilled in such a manner that the hole is larger at one end than the other. It's important to be aware of this, because it governs how you mount the bead on the hook.

With bead-head flies, the bead goes on first, before you mount the hook in the vise. This is done by inserting the point of the hook into the bead's smaller hole, so that the larger one faces to the rear once the bead has been slid into position. Debarbing abets this process.

Let's briefly revisit our soft-hackle wet fly and add a bead. You simply mount the bead ahead of time and slide it forward to the eye of the hook. Then tie the fly in the usual manner. At the end, you have the choice of wrapping the hackle behind the bead or of tying off, sliding the bead back over the tie-off wraps, then tying back on again, making the hackle, and completing the fly. Of course, you'll need to leave

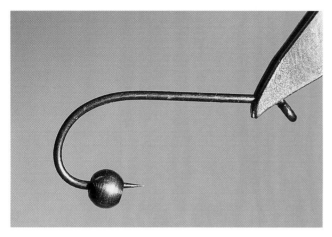

Mounting a bead on a hook.

some space up front if you opt for the latter method.

In either case, it becomes self-evident why the bead was mounted with the wide end rearward: It enables you to cover the thread wraps that immediately precede it. I suggest that you build up the thread a bit before tying off, so that the bead fits fairly snugly and is stabilized. When the bead is situated ahead of the hackle, I advocate tying on again at the eye and wrapping some thread back against the front of the bead, in order to immobilize it. You might also consider putting a small droplet of Zap-A-Gap or the like on the thread wraps before you slide the bead back over them.

Bead-head flies are amazingly effective. You can add beads to just about any soft-hackle and to nymphs and streamers as well. For example, the Hare's Ear Nymph that we'll be tying in the next chapter makes a superb bead head. I usually use a gold bead for that dressing.

Two versions of a Bead-Head Soft-Hackle: the bead behind and in front of the hackle.

Some Soft-Hackle Patterns

Note: The hooks for these flies are the same as for those in the pattern lesson. If you wish to go slightly longer on the beaded patterns (1XL), that's fine. Please refer to the hook chart in chapter 2 for specifics (see page 17).

1. PEACOCK/BROWN

BODY: Peacock herl.
RIBBING: (optional) Oval tinsel, either gold or silver.
HACKLE: Soft brown feather.

2. PHEASANT/HUN/BEAD

HEAD OR
THORAX: Copper bead.
BODY: Cock ring-necked pheasant tail fibers.
HACKLE: Hungarian partridge feather, preferably brown phase.

3. ELLIS

THORAX: Black dubbing or bead.
TAIL: (optional) Hungarian partridge, preferably gray phase.
BODY: Stripped quill from the eye of a peacock tail.
HACKLE: Hungarian partridge, preferably gray phase.

4. ORANGE FISHAWK

BODY: Orange floss or substitute.
RIBBING: Fine gold tinsel, either flat or oval.
HACKLE: Soft badger feather (cream with dark center).

5. GROUSE & GREEN

BODY: Green floss or substitute.
RIBBING: Fine gold tinsel, either flat or oval.
HACKLE: Hungarian partridge, ruffed grouse, speckled hen, or similar feather.

A bunch of soft-hackles. Clockwise from top right: Ellis, Grouse & Green, Pheasant/Hun/Bead, Peacock/Brown, Orange Fishawk.

6

The Nymph

YOU MAY ALREADY BE AWARE THAT TROUT TAKE MOST OF THEIR FOOD under water, and a very large percentage of it consists of nymph life. Technically, **nymphs** are the larval forms of mayflies and stoneflies. Caddisflies—and, in fact, all aquatic insect life that eventually becomes winged—have larval forms, but in entomological terminology, they are not properly called nymphs.

For the moment, let's consider mayfly nymphs only. According to my observations, these are less distinctive than the winged forms—or at least, I've found the trout to be less selective of nymphal life than with the imago, or subadult, forms. I believe this has to do with their drab coloration, the diffusion of the currents, and the fact that light diminishes with the depth of the water, which of course affects visibility.

The bottom line is that general nymph patterns have always been, and continue to be, very successful. And none has accounted for the deception of more trout than the redoubtable Hare's Ear. This is an ancient British pattern. Literature going back two centuries and more describes the scraping of the poll (hair and fur) from the mask of a hare and using it as dubbing.

Now there's a new term: **dubbing**. That's the modern American version; in the traditional British, it's "dubbin." On this side of the pond, we use the word as both a noun and a verb. In other words, it's the fur, and it's also the act of applying the fur to the thread, and then to the hook.

My first encounter with the Hare's Ear was in the form of a winged wet fly. That style of tying has pretty much given way to the more contemporary, and probably more entomologically accurate, nymph and emerger schools. The decline was also influenced by the relative difficulty of tying the wings. In my fledgling days, we never thought about the difficulty. It was an integral part of one's fly-tying education, and we just did it.

I still love winged wet flies and consider them a useful addition to my arsenal. It's often necessary to show the fish something different, and they don't see this sort of fly very often these days. And from a teaching standpoint, there's no better exercise in mastering the all-important pinch wrap than that of tying wet-fly wings. So we'll have a go at them in the next chapter.

But back to the Hare's Ear Nymph. We no longer have to scrape our own dubbing off of the bunnies; we now buy it prepackaged in fly shops. Quite a variety of shades and textures are available. Here, we'll stay pretty close to the traditional, which consists of a mottled, tweedy mixture of hair and fur in tans, grays, and rusts.

Having stated that it's now an over-the-counter product, I still should tell you that Hare's Ear dubbing is very easy to make—and you don't even need a bona fide English hare's mask. Common American rabbit will do, provided you have something to mix in as an additive that will imbue it with the spikiness (there's an esoteric fly-tying word) that characterizes the original. The guard hairs found along the backbone of a gray squirrel or, better still, a fox squirrel are ideal. Just cut them off and mix them with the material cut from the mask of the bunny.

Serious fur mixers usually use a coffee mill—one of those little machines that grinds up coffee beans, nuts, and such. However, the same effect can be achieved as follows:

1. In a small bowl, mix some lukewarm water with a few drops of liquid dish detergent.
2. Cut off the various furs and hairs and place them in the bowl.
3. Stir the stuff around until it is well mixed.
4. Pour the mixture into a sieve and rinse until the detergent is washed out.
5. Squeeze out as much water as you can, then lay the dubbing on a paper towel to dry.

This method works for all kinds of furs and hairs, and even for combining synthetics with natural materials. This is not always feasible in a blender, as some of the synthetics are plastic and will get gooey when zapped by the blades. Incidentally, don't try to use a conventional bottom-bladed blender; not only won't it do the job, but the material will quite possibly get bound up in the blades as well, which will destroy the motor.

The nymph we are about to tie is of typical construction, and if you can tie this one, you can tie all similar dressings. A word about the **wing case:** This is the part of the nymph's anatomy that protects the immature wings until the insect is ready to hatch out. We are going to use a narrow strip of feather from a goose or duck wing, treated with an adhesive, to emulate this component. There are other materials that also make great wing cases. Bugskin, which is actually very thin leather, is one of them. Another is Thin Skin, an interesting synthetic product from the Wapsi Company. Both are available in quite a wide range of shades and markings. As your knowledge of aquatic life develops, you'll find yourself making associations between the fly-tying materials you see and the insects you encounter astream, and these products will help you emulate what you see.

This version of the Hare's Ear Nymph is very basic and simplistic. There are a number of embellishments commonly employed by fly tyers; I'll describe a few at the end of the chapter. Incidentally, this pattern is tied both with and without gold tinsel ribbing. Here, I've included it. If you prefer to omit it, that's okay. I've also listed the wire underbody as optional, but personally, I prefer integrating weight in the tying process to having to add weight to the leader in order to get my nymphs down to fishing depths.

Before we begin, a few words about the dubbing process. There are two basic methods: single thread and double thread, or spinning loop. Here, we'll use the former. Afterward, I'll show you how the spinning-loop process goes, so you also have that method in your arsenal.

THE USE OF WAX

Some dubbings spin onto the thread very easily and smoothly, whereas others present more difficulty. For this reason, we sometimes resort to the use of a little wax. Personally, I'm not crazy about wax and seldom use it. However, I recognize that some people have very dry skin, and a touch of wax is most helpful for them. I counsel you to choose a nonsticky wax and to use it very sparingly. Sticky, or tacky, waxes tend to cause the material to adhere more to your fingers than to the thread.

Wax can be applied to the thread itself, the fingers, or both. Remember that you are probably tying with pre-waxed thread; it's the norm these days. By applying plenty of finger pressure as you spin on the dubbing material, you can create a little heat and activate the wax in the thread. If this doesn't seem to do the job, then dab a very thin coating of nontacky wax onto the forefinger of your right hand.

Notes on Single-Thread Dubbing

Please read this message before going farther. Common dubbing mistakes made by beginning tyers are:

1. Trying to apply the material in clumps, rather than wisps.
2. Uneven distribution.
3. Failing to pinch tightly enough while spinning.
4. Using too much dubbing overall.

While great dissimilarities exist between them, certain rules apply to all sorts of dubbings:

1. Tease out the material in tiny wisps.
2. Try to lay the fibers parallel to the thread.
3. Build up the "worm" of dubbing slowly, gradually, and smoothly, using small amounts.
4. While wrapping the dubbing onto the hook, if you find that you need a little more, don't wait until you've run out. Apply it while you still have a couple of wraps left on the thread, so as to effect a smooth integration. Back off a couple of turns, if necessary.

5. Conversely, if you find that you've applied too much material to the thread, back off a wrap or two, remove the excess, respin, and rewrap.

As you develop dubbing skill, you'll be able to shape the bodies of your flies any way that you want. Usually, a gradual taper is desired. With typically sized flies, this is done by simply applying the material a tiny bit thicker as you work forward. On large flies, you might apply the dubbing in layers, first wrapping forward, then spinning on more dubbing and working rearward, then spinning on yet more dubbing and working forward again.

Note: It's advisable to treat the wing-case strip with an adhesive ahead of time. Any flexible cement or glue will do, such as Pliobond, Dave's Flexament, or AquaFlex. You can coat the strips individually or simply coat the entire feather and,

HARE'S EAR NYMPH DRESSING

HOOK:	1X or 2X long, medium-gauge wire, typically sizes 8 to 16.
THREAD:	Preferably brown 6/0 or 8/0, but black is allowable.
TAIL:	A small bunch of the dubbing with guard hairs included.
UNDERBODY:	(optional) Fine lead wire or substitute.
RIBBING:	(optional) Fine oval gold tinsel.
BODY/THORAX:	Hare's Ear dubbing.
WING CASE:	A narrow strip from a gray goose or duck wing feather (see note below).
LEGS:	The dubbing, picked out a bit around the thorax.

after it's dry, separate it into strips with a needle or scissors tip. In either case, be attentive to proportions: The wing-case strip should be slightly wider than the widest part of the thorax. Have a piece of waxed paper at hand on which to lay the feather during drying. Allow for thorough drying before using the strips.

TYING STEPS

1. Tie on near the front and wrap to the bend. Then tie in the tail with a few pinch wraps, followed by several reinforcing wraps.

2. If you intend to rib the fly, tie in the tinsel now, adjacent to the tail butt.

3. Wrap the wire per instructions for the Woolly Bugger (see page 28), leaving some space in back and in front. Use the tying thread to create little "ramps" front and rear, in order to compensate for the diameter of the wire. Coat with a clear adhesive of some sort.

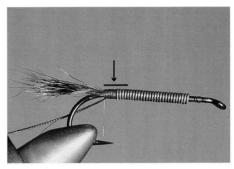

Tail, tinsel, and wire in place (steps 1-3).

4. Now for the dubbing. Position the thread a few turns ahead of the tail butt, and expose a few inches of it. Hold the bobbin in your left hand and apply tension to the thread.

5. Remember the dubbing notes. Tease out a very small puff of the dubbing material, and spin it onto the thread with your right thumb and forefinger. It's okay to spin in either direction, but don't roll the material, because the reverse motion will loosen what was spun on. I emphasize: Tease out the dubbing in tiny wisps, lay it on parallel to the thread, insofar as that's possible, and build up the dubbing a little at a time. This enables effective thread contact and a smooth application.

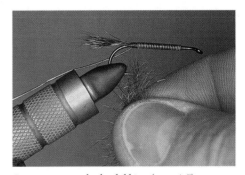

Beginning to apply the dubbing (steps 4-5).

6. Apply enough material to cover up to the middle of the thorax. Refer to photo #5 for proportions.

7. Transfer the bobbin to your tying hand and wrap to the rear, the idea being that the "worm" of material will begin to deploy around the hook precisely at the base of the tail. Then wrap progressively forward. The

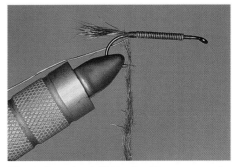

This is how the dubbing should appear on the thread (step 5).

Wrapping the dubbing (step 7).

Body completed. Note thread position (step 8).

material will tend to loosen as you wrap, so respin it as required during the process.

8. Ideally, you'll have run out of dubbing when you reach the midpoint of the thorax, which is about 20 percent of the shank length to the rear of the eye. Now wrap the thread a few turns back over the dubbed material. The reason for doing this is to create bulk over which to tie on the wing-case strip. Keep in mind that the thorax is the widest part of a nymph, both natural and artificial. Your thread should now be positioned about 35 percent of the shank length to the rear of the eye.

9. If you're doing ribbing, wrap it now, keeping the turns evenly spaced and not too close together. Tie off in the area where you wrapped back over the dubbing. Trim off the tag.

10. As I previously mentioned, the wing-case strip should be slightly wider than the widest part of the dubbed thorax. Because it will be

Ribbing in place (step 9).

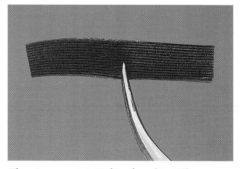

The wing-case strip tied in place (step 10).

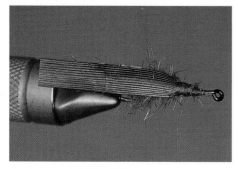

A wing-case strip (step 10).

The thorax dubbed on (step 11).

folded forward over the thorax subsequently, it is tied in by the tip or fine end, good-side down, and hanging off to the rear. "Good side" refers to the darker or exterior side of the feather. Center the strip accurately and sneak the thread over, so that it doesn't pleat or fold. Bind it in place securely, and trim off the excess.

11. Dub the thorax, using the techniques just described. Don't crowd the eye.

12. Bring the wing-case strip forward over the dubbed thorax and tie it in place. Keep it centered, and don't allow the thread action to cause it to fold back over itself. After securing it, trim off the excess, wrap a neat head, and make the whip finish.

13. With a needle, carefully pick out a little of the dubbing at the front of the thorax to simulate the legs of the insect. Then apply your lacquer to the head.

Folding the wing case into place (step 12).

The completed fly (step 13).

Notes on Spinning-Loop Dubbing

As I've mentioned, some dubbings are more difficult to work with, especially on larger flies, such as the Casual Dress pattern listed at the end of the chapter. That's where the spinning-loop dubbing method comes in handy. Here's how it goes:

1. Expose from the bobbin a little more than twice the length of thread you would normally use for the single-thread dubbing process.

2. Spin on the dubbing. You may wish to make the worm a little thicker, because the loop will pack the material tighter when it is twisted.

3. With your hackle pliers, seize the thread just below where the dubbing material ends. Hold the pliers in your left hand and keep tension on the thread.

4. Take the bobbin in your right hand and pass the thread over the hook at the point where it was hanging when you applied the dubbing. Wrap the thread forward to where the body will end.

5. Spin the hackle pliers, tightly twisting the dubbing within the loop.

6. Using the pliers as a handle, wrap the dubbing around the hook, thus forming the fly body. Respin as necessary.

Nymph Enhancement

Enhancements of nymphs of this type include the use of soft, attractively marked feathers for tails and legs. Hungarian partridge and speckled hen are two very popular types. Simply tie on a small bunch of barbs for the tail, and another for the legs. The appearance of the legs can be improved by deploying the barbs to the sides, as well as on the bottom.

Rather than apply ribbing, tyers sometimes add **flash** to their nymphs by mixing some sort of glittery material with the dubbing. This is easy to do with the detergent-and-water method described earlier (see page 42). There are plenty of high-brilliance materials that accommodate this, Lite Brite being one of them. Usually, it's necessary to chop up this material with strong scissors before doing the mixing.

My own little contribution to the embellishment of nymphs is the use of the **bead thorax.** We looked at beads in chapter 5, remember? To substitute a bead for a dubbed or fur thorax, proceed as follows:

1. Select a bead of the desired color, large enough to make a properly sized thorax on the fly you'll be tying.

2. Slide the bead onto the hook, inserting the point into the smaller hole, as described at the end of the soft-hackle chapter (see page 37), and move it to the front.

3. Tie the fly in the normal manner, but don't dub in the thorax area, and avoid excessive thread buildup. Omit the wire underbody.

4. After tying in the wing-case material, tie off, and slide the bead back over the thread wraps.

5. Tie back on in front of the bead. If you wish, and if there's enough space, add legs. Then fold the wing case forward over the bead, tie it down, and finish off the fly.

One note: When you're making bead-thorax nymphs, things work better if the wing-case material isn't too bulky. Thin Skin is a good choice. I've included in the group photo a nymph that incorporates the embellishments of a bead thorax and Hungarian partridge legs.

Some Nymph Patterns

1. PHEASANT TAIL/BEAD THORAX

HOOK:	As specified in the tying lesson.
THREAD:	Brown.
THORAX:	Copper bead.
TAIL & BODY:	Cock ring-necked pheasant tail fibers.
RIBBING:	(optional) Very fine copper wire, reverse-wrapped.
WING CASE:	Bugskin, Thin Skin, or section of goose feather treated with adhesive.
HACKLE:	Hungarian partridge, speckled hen, or cock ring-necked pheasant tail fibers.

2. AMBER FLASHBACK NYMPH

HOOK:	As specified in the tying lesson.
THREAD:	Tan, brown, or rust.
TAIL:	Brown mallard flank feather fibers or Hungarian partridge, tied fairly long.
RIBBING:	Brown Uni-Stretch, or thin floss twisted fine, or thick thread.
UNDERBODY:	(optional) Fine lead wire or substitute.
BODY/THORAX:	Amber dubbing, either natural or synthetic.
WING CASE:	Wide Mylar flat tinsel, either gold or silver.
HACKLE:	Brown mallard flank feather fibers or Hungarian partridge.

3. ZUG BUG

HOOK:	1XL or 2XL.
THREAD:	Black.
TAIL:	Three peacock sword fronds.
UNDERBODY:	(optional) Fine lead wire or substitute.
RIBBING:	Oval silver tinsel.
BODY:	Peacock herl.
LEGS:	Brown hackle fibers.
WING CASE:	Barred mallard flank feather, trimmed to shape and tied on at the head.

4. CASUAL DRESS

HOOK:	3XL or 4XL.
THREAD:	Black.
TAIL:	A small bunch of fur from the back of a muskrat, with the guard hairs left in.

An armada of nymphs. Top left: Zug Bug. Top right: Amber Flashback. Center: Casual Dress. Lower left: Black Montana. Lower right: Pheasant Tail/Bead Thorax.

UNDERBODY:	Lead wire or substitute.
BODY:	Dubbing from the back of a muskrat, with the guard hairs left in.
COLLAR:	A bunch of fur from the back of a muskrat, with the guard hairs left in.
HEAD:	Black ostrich herl or dubbing.

5. BLACK MONTANA

HOOK:	3XL or 4XL.
THREAD:	Black.
TAIL:	Black hackle.
BODY:	Black chenille.
HACKLE:	Soft black feather, wrapped over the thorax material.
THORAX:	Orange or yellow chenille.
WING CASE:	Black chenille, three strands.

Note: The hooks and thread colors for these flies vary with the designs. Please refer to the hook chart in chapter 2 (page 17) for specifics.

7

The Winged Wet Fly

HAVING BEGUN MY FLY FISHING ON THE FABLED RIVERS OF NEW YORK'S CATSKILLS, I was introduced early on to the winged wet fly. My first two fly-caught trout came to either a Leadwing Coachman or a Hare's Ear, I can't remember which. Such dressings were part of the Catskill tradition in those days, and we never questioned their effectiveness. If we weren't catching fish—well, it was our own ineptitude, or else they just weren't biting.

Or perhaps we were using the wrong pattern. Attempting to cover all bases, we often fished a three-fly cast: a tippet fly and two "droppers," as they were called. Typically, I'd tie on a Leadwing Coachman as my end fly, and a Hare's Ear and either a Dark or a Light Cahill as my dropper flies. If the fish showed a preference for any one of them, I'd cut off the others and fish three of the hot pattern!

Now that you've learned how to tie the peacock and the dubbed bodies, the next step is to learn the wet-fly wing, which is also called the **down wing**. The one we'll tie here is made out of the same sort of wing quill we used for the nymphal wing casing, but it is tied in a different manner, and there's no impregnation. Other types of down wings are made of bunches of flank fibers from birds such as the wood duck, mallard, and teal, and of small bundles of fur and hair.

In the last chapter, I mentioned that one factor in the demise of the winged wet fly was the relative difficulty of tying the wings. Don't be frightened: The key word is *relative*. These wings aren't all that tough to tie, given a little orientation and instruction, and I think you'll be very pleased with the results.

First, the orientation. Selecting a feather that's suited to the task is paramount. The flight quills from the wings of Canada geese and larger ducks are what we generally use. Those from smaller ducks are fine for winging smaller flies. The ones that form the leading edge are called **primaries** and have some useful material on them. The feathers a little farther back are called **secondaries** and are usually the best. After that come the **tertials,** which may have some decent winging material but are usually relegated to nymph wing-casing work.

Prime winging feathers have only moderate curvature and are large enough that the strips we cut out and use for the wings are long enough to be manageable and to allow us to work outside of the coarse portion near the butt end. If you inspect a typical flight quill, you'll see a sort of line that runs parallel to the quill. The material to the quill side of that line is pretty rough stuff. It's fine for holding onto during tying, but otherwise not at all tyer friendly. This is why we operate on the portion to the outside.

It is necessary to have two opposing feathers, meaning a right and a left. The closer they are in size, shape, and texture, the easier your task will be.

The most common wing mistakes that beginners make include:

1. Using strips that are too wide and, less frequently, ones that are too narrow.
2. Poor selection of feathers.
3. Failure to lay down a proper thread base before tying on the wings.
4. Crowding the front of the body.
5. Poor technique with the pinch wrap.
6. Failure to mount the winging strips in proper position.
7. Tying on the strips upside down.
8. Upsetting the finished wings while trimming the butts.

That's quite a list, but don't let it unnerve you. All of these problems are easily solvable; I'll go into all that in detail as we tie the fly. As to selection of feathers, I've already touched on that.

One other item that I'll address here is the matter of what right-side up means, with reference to the winging strips. Picture the feather standing up in front of you, with the butt end of the quill on the table. A strip cut with the feather in this position is considered right-side up. This is sometimes referred to as **pointed-end up.**

Sometimes, looking at finished flies can be deceptive, especially in the case of feather-winged salmon flies. This is because the tyer has manipulated the winging strips in such a manner that it appears as though they were tied on with the bottom, or curvy, edges upward. Actually, what happened was that the tyer "humped" the strips, thus altering their configuration. You'll see how this is done in the tying sequence.

Okay, why pointed-end up? The reason is that if the strips are tied on upside down, the pressure of the thread has a tendency to work against the texture of the strips, causing the fibers to separate. You may not encounter this while tying the fly, but you may well see it evidenced after a few casts. So while there are a few exceptions, we generally tie on our winging strips pointed-end up.

Since both the Leadwing Coachman and the Hare's Ear take the same wings, we could do either or both, based on what we've already covered. I've chosen to show you the Leadwing here. In either case, it's important that the wings not be

LEADWING COACHMAN DRESSING	
HOOK:	Typical wet fly, standard or 1XL shank length, typically sizes 10 to 14.
THREAD:	Black 6/0 or 8/0.
TAG:	Narrow flat gold tinsel.
BODY:	Peacock herl.
HACKLE:	Soft dark brown barbs, tied as a beard.
WINGS:	Gray goose or duck, as described.

interfered with by the front of the body. This implies not ending the body too far forward or making it too bulky. It also means laying down an adequate thread base.

In addition to the lesson in wings, which is the main thrust of this chapter, we'll examine the simple beard hackle commonly found on this type of fly. Let me discuss this briefly. Remember the discourse on folding a feather late in the soft-hackle chapter (see page 36), and my statement that this was an important technique that would be used in many fly-tying operations? This is one of them. This is good practice for working on dry-fly tails in forthcoming exercises.

The procedure starts out the same way as was described. Stroke the barbs on a feather to 90 degrees from the quill. Now either cut or pull them off in a bunch, being careful to keep the tips even. A note here: Some feathers are symmetrical—the length of the barbs is the same on both sides of the quill—whereas some are not. With symmetrical feathers, you can gather barbs from both sides of the quill at once by stroking them all together as you would when folding a feather. However, if the barb lengths differ, use only one side at a time; otherwise, the tips won't come out even.

There's also a little tag of gold tinsel, but that's pretty much a no-brainer. I should tell you that there are variations of this pattern, as there are of so many. This is one of several that were popular in the Catskills when I was getting started.

TYING STEPS

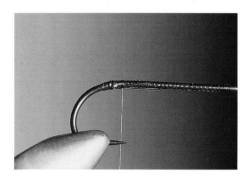

The tinsel tag tied in place (steps 1-2)

Peacock body completed, beard hackle being measured (steps 3-5).

Tying in the beard with an upside-down pinch (step 6).

1. Tie on near the front and wrap to the bend. Then tie in a piece of narrow flat tinsel with the gold side against the hook shank. Why? Because this material has a tendency to flip over with the first wrap, and we want the gold side to face outward! Trim off the excess.

2. Make a small tag, using just a few turns, working just a bit down around the bend and back. Secure and trim the tinsel.

3. Either tie in a 5- or 6-inch (125 to 150 mm) piece of thread, or make a loop of that length and cut off one side of it, whichever is easier for you. This, of course, is the reinforcing thread for the peacock. Why didn't we simply leave the excess thread hanging as we did before? Because it gets in the way when the tinsel tag is being tied!

4. Construct a peacock herl body, following the instructions in the soft-hackle exercise (see page 34). Don't crowd the front; refer to the photo for proportions.

5. Per instructions in the discourse on folding a feather and gathering barbs, procure the hackle material (see page 35). Gather and either cut or pull off a small bunch, being careful to keep the tips even.

6. Hold the bunch beneath the hook—at the throat, so to speak. Tie it in with a few upside-down pinch wraps, secure with several more tight wraps, and carefully trim off the excess.

7. Working very carefully and neatly, wrap a thread base on which to mount the wings, as shown. End up with the thread a bit ahead of the front of the body, but not abutting it.

8. Cut a section from each of the two flight feathers—the left and the right. The closer to identical, the better. As to width: I'm working on a size 10 hook, and the strips are about $3/16$ to $7/32$ inch (6 to 7 mm) wide.

9. Match the sections with the concave sides facing inward, so that the respective curvatures cancel each other out, and the wing strips are straight and flat. They need to be perfectly aligned.

10. Hold the wing set with your right thumb and forefinger and place it atop the hook. The wings should extend rearward until the tips touch, or barely break, an imaginary line that runs straight upward from the rear extremity of the bend of the hook.

11. With your left thumb and forefinger, hump the wing set slightly by stroking the tips downward. This establishes the desired shape and counteracts the effect the thread will have during tie-on.

12. Transfer the wing set to your left hand. Place the feathers precisely atop the hook and reestablish the length. Make sure they are perfectly centered and aligned with the hook shank.

13. Sneak the thread up between your fingers, then over the wing set, and between your fingers again on the far side of the hook. Execute your class-A pinch wrap, crushing the wing set down onto the thread base. Repeat this several times. Do not allow the torque action of the thread to move the wings off center. Keep pressure against the far side of the hook with your left index finger, in order to prevent the wings from slipping downward.

    Note: Some people find it helpful, with the first pinch wrap, to come under the hook and sneak the thread up under the fingers a second time, then tighten by pulling upward. If you have trouble, you might give this technique a try.

14. Inspect what you've done. If the wings are not positioned as desired, back off the thread wraps and do the process over again. If they are correctly positioned, seize them with your left hand again, hold them steady, and secure them with several firm wraps of

Beard in place, thread base wrapped in preparation for the wing (step 7).

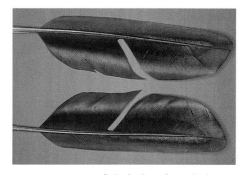

Two opposing goose flight feathers from which a set of winging strips have been removed (step 8).

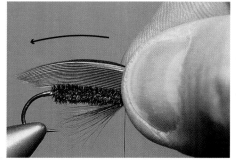

Winging strips in position for being tied on (steps 9-11).

Tying on the wings with a series of pinch wraps (steps 12-15).

thread. Keep in mind that there is still thread torque happening, which can alter the position of the wings. Don't let this take place.

15. Inspect the wings again, and adjust, if necessary. Remember: Until you have trimmed them off, the wing butts can be used as handles for making subtle adjustments.

16. With the tips of your sharpest scissors, cut off the wing butts flush with the thread wraps. Hold the wings firmly in place while cutting, because the shearing action of the scissors can also work to upset the wing position. Use several chops, instead of trying to cut everything at once, which would exacerbate shearing action.

17. While still holding the wings, cover the trimmed butts with a few more wraps. Then do the whip finish, and sit back and admire the beautiful fly you've just created.

The completed Leadwing Coachman (steps 16-17).

There are literally hundreds of wet-fly patterns out there, using all sorts of materials for wings, bodies, hackle, highlights, and so forth. As mentioned, one of the all-time greats is the Hare's Ear. My favorite version of it uses either Hungarian partridge or speckled hen barbs for the tail and hackle, these being very similar materials. The gold rib is optional. I've included the dressing in the group that follows.

Some Wet-Fly Patterns

1. DARK CAHILL

TAIL: Medium brown barbs.
BODY: Gray dubbing.
HACKLE: Soft brown, beard-style.
WINGS: Barred wood duck flank or dyed imitation.

2. LIGHT CAHILL

TAIL: Cream barbs.
BODY: Cream dubbing or yarn.
HACKLE: Soft cream, beard-style.
WINGS: Barred wood duck flank or dyed imitation.

3. BLACK GNAT

TAIL: (optional) Black barbs.
BODY: Black chenille, yarn, or dubbing.
HACKLE: Soft black, beard-style.
WINGS: Dark goose wing quill sections.

4. BROWN TURKEY

TAIL: None.
HACKLE: Brown rooster, wrapped palmer-style over the body from the bend to the throat.
BODY: Brown floss, yarn, Uni-Stretch, or the like.
WINGS: Mottled brown turkey sections.

5. HARE'S EAR

THREAD: Preferably brown 6/0 or 8/0, but black is allowable.
TAIL: A small bunch of either Hungarian partridge or speckled hen barbs.
RIBBING: (optional) Fine oval gold tinsel.
BODY: Hare's Ear dubbing.
HACKLE: Hungarian partridge or speckled hen barbs, beard-style.
WINGS: Sections from opposing gray goose or duck wing quills. The gold rib is optional.

Note: The hooks for these patterns are the same as for the tying lesson. Please refer to the hook chart in chapter 2 for specifics (page 17).

A covey of wet flies. Top left: Dark Cahill. Top right: Brown Turkey. Center: Light Cahill. Lower left: Hare's Ear. Lower right: Black Gnat.

8

The Hair-Winged Streamer

PERHAPS THE MOST UNDERUSED TYPE OF FLY IN ALL OF fly fishing is the streamer. It is intended to imitate, or at least to suggest, some sort of baitfish. The two general categories are the **imitator** and the **attractor,** or suggestive type. That's for the convenience of us humans. Fish are not admirers of the fly tyer's craft. To them, there's no such thing as an "attractor." They think it's real food, or they would never try to eat it.

Streamers are also divided into other subgroups that are defined by the primary material used for the main part of the silhouette. This is called the **wing,** which of course is a complete misnomer, as baitfish don't have wings. However, since the component goes on in the same position as would a wet-fly wing, we call it by that name. In actuality, it's the upper part of the body of the baitfish, if indeed it's anything identifiable at all.

The most common of these subgroups are the **hairwings** and the **featherwings.** The latter includes streamers with marabou wings. The former includes a large number of patterns that are tied with all sorts of hair. Some of them are called bucktails, because the original dressings used deer tail hair, which is still probably the most commonly used material in streamer tying.

If you're anything like me, you'll enjoy streamer tying, because to a large degree it releases you from the disciplines of imitative tying. Much of the time, you'll be working on large hooks with pretty materials that are easy and fun to use. I also hope that you'll give them a fair workout on the water. My basic method of fishing a streamer is to keep it moving and swimming in a lifelike manner, but with little pauses, so that the predator fish gets the idea that this morsel is easily catchable. I think you'll find the results truly exciting.

The first fly I ever tied was a bucktail called the Mickey Finn. It's still a popular and effective fly today, and no one is exactly sure why, because it certainly bears no resemblance to any natural baitfish a trout might encounter. Apparently the answer lies in the visibility of the fly, which uses the two colors that are best seen under water, plus some silver flash.

Today, various hairs other than bucktail have become popular. Recently, I've begun to see goat hair of several types arriving from Scandinavia, along with arctic fox, both body and tail hair. These are very nice materials to work with and have justifiably gained favor. Certain sheep also produce hair that is suitable for streamer work. Calf tail is sometimes used, but I don't favor it for this particular design of streamer, because even the straightest calf tail is rather crinkly, which makes it hard to obtain the well-defined layers and slender silhouette that I strive for.

More important than the actual variety of animal from which the hair comes is its texture. For smaller streamers—"trout sized," as they are often called—you'll want finely textured hair from a smaller bucktail. (Incidentally, while I'm not going to try to change the terminology that's developed over the past century, it would be more appropriate to refer to this material as deer tail, since we have no way of knowing whether it came from the male or female of the species.)

While bucktail is often used in its natural coloration, the stuff we are using here is, quite obviously, dyed. Today's suppliers have, for the most part, learned how to dye such materials very well indeed, which wasn't always the case when I first tied the Mickey. Look for bright, uniform coloration when selecting tails. If you find that the dye readily comes off on your fingers while tying, you might point this out to your dealer.

I depart from the original dressing in one respect: I use embossed tinsel instead of flat ribbed with oval. This is flat tinsel with little indentations patterned into it, which are quite suggestive of the scales of a small fish. I feel that the embossed tinsel yields a more attractive effect and is far more durable than the relatively delicate oval. However, if you want to be faithful to the traditional dressing, that's fine with me, in which case I suggest that you use a fairly substantial oval tinsel for the ribbing.

All flat tinsels, including the embossed type, are usually applied in two layers, meaning that they are tied in near the front and wrapped to the rear and back, so as to hide any little spaces between wraps. That's what we'll do here. However, if at some point in the future you want to use a single layer of embossed tinsel for this type of body, and have acquired sufficient skill to cover the hook efficiently and smoothly, that's fine. You'll need to overlap the edges very slightly. This is helpful on small streamers, where you're trying to avoid too much bulk. Several widths of embossed tinsel are available. Except for very small streamers, I prefer wide tinsel, as it goes on more smoothly and with fewer turns.

Today, softer alloys are being used in the manufacture of embossed tinsels, the Uni Products version being a prime example. This material is much less lethal and is easier to work with than the old metallic stuff. Still, you must be careful not to run the thread along the edge of embossed tinsel, because it has sawlike properties.

I want to mention one more difference between the original flat-and-oval configuration and the embossed version. When you're using the former, I advocate finishing the body well short of the eye of the hook and tying off the oval ribbing underneath the shank. This avoids interference with the wing. With the embossed type, I find it helpful to work forward with a couple of turns of tinsel ahead of the tie-in point and then to apply a smooth thread base and set the wings at this spot. In this manner, I avoid the wing hairs' being cocked upward by the front of the body. It's desirable that the wing lie flat along the top of the hook.

I have one particular technique that might be considered a departure from traditional wisdom. When possible, I like to wrap flat and embossed tinsels over a bare hook. This allows the material to slide into place in perfectly adjacent turns. The fact that the wraps, if properly done, abut each other prevents them from slipping around during fishing. However, many streamers have tails, butts, or something else that must be tied in at the rear, which disallows wrapping the body material over the bare hook shank. This brings certain thread- and materials-management disciplines into play. I'll explain further after we tie the Mickey.

A word about hooks for streamers. Usually, a long-shanked model is called for. This allows you to closely emulate the shape of a small fish. It also enables the positioning of the "wing" material in such a manner that it won't tangle around the hook shank so readily during casting. If the wings are tied too long, such tangling can be a problem, especially when soft materials such as marabou are used.

Several manufacturers offer streamer hooks with what is called a **looped eye.** In this design, the wire that forms the eye is brought back down the shank a little way, rather than stubbed off at the closure of the eye. Two things are thus accomplished: The potential for a rough edge at the eye is eliminated, and a double-wire base is established. This can be very helpful in mounting wing materials on streamers, both hair and feather.

There are a couple of downsides. First, the return wire, as it is called, must be well tapered and must lie adjacent to the main shank; otherwise, there's a bump that's difficult to work around during tying. The other factor is that properly made looped-eye hooks can be a bit pricey. Personally, I feel the advantages offset the negatives, and I tend to favor looped-eye hooks for streamer work.

MICKEY FINN DRESSING

HOOK:	A longer-shanked (4XL to 7XL) model, as shown; typically sizes 4 to 12.
THREAD:	Black 6/0 or 8/0.
BODY:	Silver embossed tinsel.
WING:	Yellow and red hair (bucktail or similar), configured according to the instructions to follow.

While on the subject of hook eyes, let me briefly address the matter of design, meaning turned down, turned up, or straight. I prefer either a turned-down or straight eye, as I feel that a turned-up eye may cause the streamer to plane like a water ski in the current. However, I would counsel you to avoid hooks with eyes that are too sharply turned down. About 30 degrees is a good turn-down angle. This allows you to use whatever knot you want for attaching the fly to the leader: either the **turle knot,** which is formed around the neck of the fly behind the eye, or the **improved clinch knot,** which sets ahead of the eye. Hooks with a radical turn-down angle may cause the fly to behave erratically in the water.

With that, let's tie a Mickey Finn, adhering to the original design and proportions, with the exception of the aforementioned embossed tinsel.

TYING STEPS

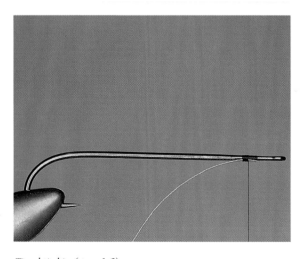

Tinsel tied in (steps 1-3).

1. Be sure your vise is properly adjusted for the size—meaning the wire diameter—of your hook. Long-shanked hooks have a tendency to work loose in the jaws of the vise, due to their inherent increased leverage.
2. Tie on near the eye and wrap neatly rearward a little way. Refer to the photo for dimensions.
3. Cut off a piece of tinsel of sufficient length to allow you to wrap two layers and still have enough left at the end for easy handling. In the case of a size 6, 6XL hook, this would be about 6 or 7 inches (150 to 175 mm). Tie it in lengthwise with the shank beneath the hook, and wrap neatly

forward, using one layer of thread, avoiding the buildup of bulk. Trim off the tag end of the tinsel and bind it down. The thread should now be positioned as shown in the photo.

4. Start the tinsel by folding it over itself. This forms a little "pleat," which you can flatten and smooth out with your fingernail or with flat-jawed pliers or tweezers, if necessary. This brings the tinsel into wrapping position.

5. Wrap rearward, using the following technique: Overlap the wraps very slightly, then with the next turn let the previous wrap slip down off the edge into an adjacent position. You'll hear and feel a little click as this happens. This produces smooth, uniform turns.

6. When you reach the bend of the hook, start working forward over the first layer. Use the same overwrap-and-slip-off technique.

7. When you reach the tie-in point, wrap past it two or three turns. This is a single layer, so be attentive to making the wraps abut, with no space between.

8. Tie off the tinsel against the bottom of the hook. This is the most dangerous time with regard to cutting the thread, so be careful to work against the flat of the tinsel, and don't let the thread scrape along the edge.

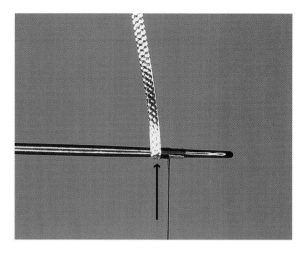

Starting the tinsel by crimping it into this position (step 4).

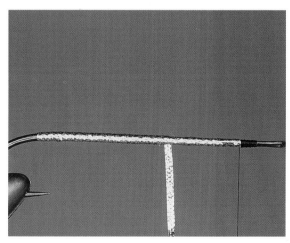

Wrapping the tinsel (steps 5-6).

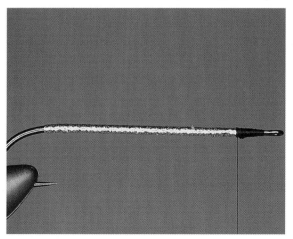

The finished tinsel body, thread base wrapped preparatory to winging (steps 7-9).

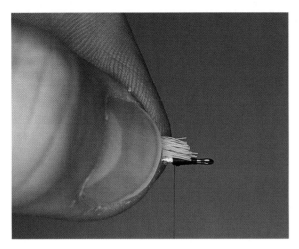

The first bunch of hair, pretrimmed to length (steps 10-12).

The first layer of hair in place, new thread base established (steps 13-14).

9. Trim off the excess tinsel, then lay down a smooth thread base, using two or three layers of thread, working up to the hook eye, then back over the single layers of tinsel a little. The idea is to establish a perfectly flat base on which to tie the hair.

10. Prepare the first layer of hair as follows: Cut off a small bunch of the yellow hair (check the photos for proportions), and prune out any and all the underfur and short hairs. You can do this with your fingers by holding the hair bunch by its tip end and stroking toward its butt end. A fine-toothed comb makes this even easier. Also, prune out any aberrant hairs that are too long, twisty, or curly. However, don't use a stacker to neaten up the tips, because this produces a whisk-broom effect and results in a chopped-off image that doesn't suggest the streamlined silhouette of a small fish.

11. Establish the length of the hair by setting it atop the hook and observing how far the tips extend beyond the rear of the bend. I suggest that this dimension be about one-third of the shank length, and definitely no more than one-half. Then transfer the bunch to your left hand.

12. You now have a choice: You can tie the bunch onto the hook as is and trim the butts later, or you can pretrim to length now. I prefer the latter method, but if you opt for it, care must be taken. Make sure you've established the proper length. When trimming the butts, slope-cut them slightly, but not too much, or you won't have enough material on top to enable a secure tie-down.

13. With the hair bunch sitting flat on top of the thread base and perfectly aligned with the hook shank, tie it on by sneaking a couple of soft wraps over the bunch, followed by a series of very firm ones. Make sure all the hair stays on top of the hook.

14. Establish another thread base as you did the first one, meanwhile binding down the butt end of the first hair bunch.

15. Cut off a small bunch of the red hair equal in thickness to the yellow, and manicure it as instructed in step 10. Then repeat the tie-in process, pretrimming or not as you choose. Be sure to mount the hair on the thread base, and don't let it mix with the first bunch; a red stripe is what you want. You'll need to ramp back and forth a little near the eye, in order to shape the front end properly and to avoid having too severe a slope. In the process, establish yet another thread base.

16. Cut off a second bunch of yellow hair somewhat thicker than the first. The traditional dressing specifies that it should be equal to the first two bunches combined, but that gets pretty tough to manage, so you'll need to use some discretion here. If the first two layers appear to be on the thick side, be a little conservative with the top layer, or you'll have a battle on your hands. It takes a little practice to learn how to properly proportion streamer materials. The initial tendency is to make the bunches too thick.

17. Tie on the top bunch, again working on the thread base but not wrapping rearward too far to cause the hairs to mix instead of layer.

18. Neaten, smooth out, and shape the head with discrete thread wraps, whip-finish, and apply at least two coats of head lacquer. Instructions for adding eyes follow. If you decide to do this, you may wish to build up the head a bit before tying off, depending on the size of the head at the end of your tying process.

The red layer of hair in place, new thread base established (step 15).

The completed Mickey Finn (steps 16-18).

Adding Eyes

Adding eyes to streamers of this type has always been popular and, with the recent advent of several new types of materials, has become even more so. The traditional method is to paint on the eyes, and that works just fine, though it's somewhat time consuming. You must work on a smooth base—specifically, the aforementioned head lacquer, completely dried. You'll need two colors of lacquer, yellow and black, and two cylindrical applicators, one considerably smaller in diameter than the other. These could be round toothpicks or matchsticks cut to size. However, the rear ends of small drill bits work better than anything I've yet found. Here's the process:

1. Work on the edge of a table, or some similar place; the head of your fly must hang off an edge.
2. Shake the yellow lacquer well. With the larger of the applicators, dip into the lacquer, collecting a globule.
3. Carefully apply the globule to the head of the fly. If you have just the right amount of lacquer, the globule will spread out into a perfect circle without the applicator quite touching the head itself.
4. With the head of the fly extending off the edge of the working surface, complete the other side of the head, creating a mirror image. Set the fly aside and allow the lacquer to dry completely.
5. Shake the black lacquer well. Then, using the smaller applicator, repeat the dotting process, centering a black pupil in the yellow. Allow for thorough drying, then cover with a protective coat of clear lacquer.

A word about the relative proportions of the two applicators. The one you use for the black lacquer needs to be about half the size of the one used for the pupil. In other words, if a $1/8$-inch drill bit is the right size for the yellow, use a $1/16$-inch bit for the black.

Fairly recently, stick-on eyes became available, these being a spin-off from the lure-making industry. There are several types, some made of Mylar, others of a different synthetic. They come in many sizes and colors and are very easy to use. They won't stick to the head of a fly simply by virtue of the adhesive on their backsides, so an effective protective coating is a necessity. This could be clear epoxy or some other tough adhesive that goes on fairly thick. More about this in a bit.

A consideration. If you've been working with waxed thread, you may find that stick-on eyes don't adhere to the head of the fly very well. All that needs to happen is that they stay in place until you apply the protective coating. That probably won't be a problem, but if becomes one, simply apply one coat of clear lacquer as a base, and let it dry before sticking the eyes on.

Here's the procedure for affixing the stick-on eyes:

1. Have the fly mounted in the vise. With tweezers, peel off an eye from the sheet on which they come, and press it onto the fly head. Do the same on the far side.

2. If you're going to use epoxy, mix it well, per the instructions on the package. Using a toothpick, lay a generous blob of adhesive on the top of the head. Help it flow evenly over both sides, covering the eyes and the head entirely.

3. For a few moments, you'll have to keep an eye on things and clean off any excess adhesive that collects below the head with your toothpick. Then allow the adhesive to dry completely.

A few notes on epoxy. Make sure you get the clear stuff. I recommend against using two-part rod finishes, because they are too runny. Either the regular or the five-minute type is okay, though the latter doesn't allow much working time. For efficiency's sake, get a group of flies ready to go before mixing the epoxy, and do them all at once. You'll need something to secure them on, as only one can go into your vise. Typically, I do six at a time, because this is about as many as I can keep an eye on at once.

If you can tie the Mickey Finn, you can also tie quite a number of pretty and effective hair-winged streamers. One of the most enduring and popular is the Black-Nosed Dace. This pattern was originated before World War II by Art Flick, a legendary angler and author from New York's Catskills. It falls into the imitator group—it's designed to suggest the baitfish of the same name. However, the fact that this minnow

A Black-Nosed Dace with painted eyes.

WATER-BASED LACQUERS

Recently, a group of new water-based head lacquers appeared on the scene, put out by a company called BT Products. It offers several colors and also two types of clear: a hard finish and a flexible finish. I was pleasantly surprised to find that the flexible stuff works quite well for coating fly heads as just described. It certainly doesn't have the strength and impregnability of epoxy, but I deem it adequate for the task, and it's a most convenient and quick substitute. One coat will do; two is even better. Again, you'll have to watch out for adhesion to waxed thread—which, incidentally, is also true with epoxy. A coat of well-thinned clear head lacquer solves this problem.

is not found in many watersheds outside the Northeast and Midwest does not seem to alter its effectiveness. A friend of mine who guides on the Bighorn in Montana reports that it's a great fly there, despite the fact that there's probably no natural BNDs within a thousand miles.

I mention this because before leaving the subject of streamers, I want to elaborate on what I stated earlier about wrapping tinsel and certain other body materials over bare steel. The Black-Nosed Dace dressing calls for a tag made of red yarn. This precludes wrapping over bare hook; however, it presents an excellent opportunity to use the technique you learned earlier for adding a tag to the Woolly Worm. It is most helpful in streamer tying, and wet flies and salmon flies as well, and can be employed anytime you encounter a pattern that has a tag or tail of a material long enough and of the right texture to allow you to tie it in near the front and bind it down to the rear. To review:

1. Tie on as you would for the Mickey.
2. Cut off a piece of red yarn sufficiently longer than the hook shank so that you can grip it from the rear. Tie it in atop the hook about 20 to 25 percent to the rear of the eye, and trim off the tag end.
3. While holding it tightly from the rear, bind it neatly to the hook shank, working all the way to the bend. Then wrap neatly forward, cover the tag at the tie-in spot, and complete the fly. At some point, cut the tag to length. It should be just a short little stump.

BLACK-NOSED DACE DRESSING

HOOK,
THREAD,
& BODY: As for the Mickey Finn.
TAG: As just described.
WING: Hair in three layers. From the bottom up: white, then black to form a narrow stripe, then brown approximately equal to the white and black combined.

The universe of streamer flies is a very large and diverse one. Broadly defined, it includes the Atlantic salmon flies, certain steelhead flies, and many of our saltwater patterns, the tying techniques and materials of all being at least generally similar. For the versatile angler, this is a very important school of fly tying, and one I hope you'll find interesting and enjoyable.

Some Streamer Patterns

1. Warden's Worry

TAIL:	Two opposing sections of red-dyed goose, tied like a wet-fly wing.
RIBBING:	Flat gold tinsel.
BODY:	Fuzzy orange yellow yarn or dubbing.
THROAT HACKLE:	Yellow barbs.
WING:	Natural tan or light brown bucktail.

A school of streamers. From the top: Light Edson Tiger, Warden's Worry, Marabou Black Ghost, Llama, Dark Edson Tiger.

2. MARABOU BLACK GHOST

TAIL:	A bunch of yellow hackle fibers.
RIBBING:	Flat silver tinsel.
BODY:	Black floss or stretch nylon.
THROAT HACKLE:	Yellow hackle barbs.
WING:	White marabou.
CHEEKS:	(optional) Jungle cock or substitute.

3. LLAMA

TAIL:	Hen grizzly hackle barbs.
RIBBING:	Oval gold tinsel.
BODY:	Red floss or stretch nylon.
WING:	A bunch of woodchuck body hair, with the guards hairs left in.
HACKLE:	Soft grizzly tied as a collar.

4. EDSON TIGER, LIGHT

THREAD:	Yellow.
TAIL:	The tip of a barred black and white wood duck feather.
BODY:	Peacock herl.
WING:	Yellow bucktail or similar hair.
WING TOPPING:	A short section of red goose or duck.
CHEEKS:	Jungle cock or substitute, tied short.

5. EDSON TIGER, DARK

THREAD:	Yellow.
TAIL:	Two yellow hackles tips, tied short.
BODY:	Yellow chenille.
THROAT:	Two red hackle tips or a small red beard hackle.
WING:	A bunch of hair from the brown portion of a yellow-dyed bucktail.
CHEEKS:	Jungle cock or substitute, tied short.

Note: All of these flies are tied on streamer hooks of various lengths. They may all be tied with black thread, with the exception of the Edson Tigers, which call for yellow thread.

9

Introducing
the Dry Fly

DRY-FLY FISHING IS EASILY THE MOST POPULAR FORM OF THE SPORT, while not necessarily the most effective at all times. Fortunately, it's sufficiently productive that those who embrace the puritan ethic are not victims of asceticism, per se. And I do not use the term *ethic* in the moral sense. Despite what a certain faction within the fly-fishing fraternity might think, choice of angling method has absolutely nothing to do with either ethics or morality.

The truth is that dry-fly fishing is just sheer joy. I do a lot of subsurface fishing with all sorts of creations, but if I had my druthers, I'd be fishing dry all the time. The fact that I don't is an expression of my Dutch-German practicality.

The most common design of dry fly—what many refer to as the classic, or Catskill, school—consists of four basic components: wings, tail, body, and hackle. This is where we encounter hackle in its purest and most hallowed form: the stiff, glossy fibers that imbue our beloved dry flies with form and function. In the broadest definition, however, any fly that is fished on or in the surface can be considered a dry fly. Some of these do not, and are not intended to, imitate a winged form in either the subadult (dun) or adult (imago) stage. Rather, they are intended to suggest an insect struggling to reach that stage, and perhaps doing so unsuccessfully. Thus we have the floating emerger and stillborn dun schools. And we have imitators of terrestrial insects as well.

As I related in the streamer chapter, we have that very fuzzy dichotomy between so-called imitators and attractors. Actually, with the exception of virtual laboratory models tied as objects of art, the dry flies we fish with don't look a whole lot like the real bugs. However, the visual distortions caused by water and the manner in which light interacts with it, and the effect of the movement of currents, compensate in a very real sense for the dissimilarities. These factors also discipline fly design and the selection and use of materials. It's not so much what the fly looks like in the vise; it's how it performs on the water.

Without going into excruciating detail, let's examine the nature of **dry-fly hackle** and its quality points. From a functional standpoint, particularly with regard to the classic design, the job of the hackle is to support and float the fly on the surface of the water. It also lends coloration, shape, size, an impressionistic image, and the general illusion of a natural insect.

Here are the main attributes to look for in dry-fly hackle feathers:

1. A fine, flexible quill.
2. Stiff, strong barbs, relatively web-free.
3. High barb count—that is, a dense deployment of barbs on the quill.
4. Long "sweet spots," meaning quality throughout a large portion of the feather.
5. Consistency of barb length, which is what determines size.
6. Beautiful coloration, or sheen.

These attributes will become more meaningful as you develop your tying skills. I might comment further on the matter of **web,** as it has long been a major factor in hackle quality. This is the soft portion of a feather near the quill. In top-quality feathers, it may not be present at all, or at least not in the portion that constitutes prime hackle. If present in quantity, it's quite visible; you can see the web line running lengthwise along the quill. If there's a significant amount of it, that's bad, and you should avoid using such feathers for dry-fly work. A little web is tolerable.

There are some other considerations that pertain as much or more to making prudent purchases as to actual hackle quality or characteristics. An excellent case in point is the Hoffman line of saddle hackle, produced by Whiting Farms of Delta, Colorado. The grading system—#1, #2, #3, and so forth—is based almost entirely on the number of feathers on a pelt and their length. Feather quality, as defined above, is virtually the same throughout the three grades. So it comes down to how many flies can be tied from that pelt.

Having mentioned saddles, I should quickly sidetrack to describe **necks,** or **capes** (these two terms may be used interchangeably). Necks, which have long been the standard source of dry-fly hackle, are just what they sound like: the necks of roosters. They have been developed to a very high level of quality over the past several decades by such growers as Henry Hoffman, Ted Hebert, and Dr. Tom Whiting, who now raises both the Hoffman and Hebert strains. Necks are characterized by having a large range of hackle sizes. A top-grade cape might yield feathers for as many as eight or nine sizes of fly, from large size 10s to tiny size 24s and 26s. Material for tails may also be found on the larger feathers around the edges.

With cape feathers, we look for a long **sweet spot,** which is that portion of the feather that yields prime hackle. It is defined as follows:

1. Uniformity of barb length.
2. Relative absence of web at the center.
3. Narrow, flexible quill.

When you're tying with neck hackles, you must strip off everything that isn't part of the sweet spot; otherwise, you're simply crowding the hook with poorer-quality hackle and thicker quill, and there will be no space left for the prime stuff. Many tyers, beginners in particular, have a tendency to try to use as much of the feather as possible; it's a projection of the "I-paid-for-it-and-by-golly-I'm-going-to-use-it" mind-set. Please don't do this to yourself. Be assiduous in your assessment of each and every cape feather, and strip down to the sweet spot without compromise. Usually, this means discarding half or more of the feather. That's not a bad thing; it's to your great advantage to do so.

Saddles come from that part of the chicken where you would mount the saddle in order to ride the animal, if such were possible. Years ago, saddle feathers were seldom suitable for dry-fly work. However, with the careful and informed development of genetic hackle in recent years, saddles have caught up to, and in several respects passed, cape hackle. The feathers are long; in prime saddles, very long, sometimes exceeding a foot (30 cm) in length. On top-grade saddles, almost the entire length of the feather is of dry-fly quality, and most of the feathers on the pelt are of such quality. In other words, almost the whole feather is one huge sweet spot. The very best feathers are found along the sides of the saddle patch. There are usually some softer ones in the center, which make very good Woolly Bugger hackle.

Quality saddle feathers rate very high with respect to the points mentioned earlier. They usually have thin quills, and an extremely high barb count, which translates to more hackle per wrap. This enables you to get several or more flies out of one feather. In fact, I've gotten as many as a dozen in sizes 14 and 16 from a single feather. This is what justifies the price of such pelts.

Another great advantage of such long feathers is the ease with which they are handled. Usually, you don't need to resort to the use of hackle pliers until the feather is virtually used up, and you're down to the tip. It is also possible to wrap two feathers at the same time, thus obtaining a mix, such as that called for in the Adams and many other patterns. The fineness of the quills facilitates this.

At this point you might be wondering: Why use necks at all? There are several reasons. First, saddles have a very limited range of sizes—three at the most. They don't tie down to the very small sizes that, as you'll find out eventually, can be of great importance to the fly fisher. They do not yield tailing material, nor do they yield tippets for the wings that many patterns require. So both capes and saddles have their place in your war chest.

Another difference between necks and saddles is that with necks, unless you're tying smaller flies, you'll usually need to use two feathers. With very high-quality cape hackles, you might be able to obtain sufficient hackle with one feather for a size 14, but usually you have to get down to a 16 or 18 before this is true. With top-grade saddle feathers, one feather will usually do the trick, the reasons being (1) the extraordinarily high barb count, (2) the strength of the barbs, and (3) the ultrafine quill, which enables tighter packing.

Before we move on to our first dry-fly pattern, a few closing thoughts on hackle selection. In addition to applying the aforementioned criteria when evaluating a cape or saddle, look for aberrations. This is of particular importance when choosing saddles. Sometimes you'll encounter a saddle that has shorter barbs on one side of the quills than the other. If this difference is modest, it's not a big problem. However, if the disparity is significant, and a lot of the feathers display it, don't buy the saddle.

Also, you should be aware that the occasional long saddle feather will change sizes in the middle. In rare cases, I've encountered three different sizes on one feather! If the quality is good in other respects, go ahead and use the saddle; just keep an eye on how the size runs. If it suddenly changes to larger or smaller than you want, switch to another feather, laying the initial one aside for later use on a different-sized fly.

One more aberration to watch out for in saddles is what I call **cupping.** This refers to feathers that manifest an inward curvature of the barbs. A little of this is tolerable, but not much. Stay away from saddles that have more than a slight amount of cupping.

I'd like to begin the dry-fly section of the book with a style of dry fly that represents the ultimate in simplicity: the Bivisible. It has only two components, both of which are hackle feathers wrapped around a fine-wire hook. The second, or frontal, hackle is always white, which gives the fly its "bivisibility." The other, or main, hackle can be any color you desire.

A word about sizing hackle. The size of fly for which a particular feather is proper is determined by the length of the barbs *in the wrapped position.* Thus, when gauging the size of a feather, you must flex it into a simulation of that wrapped position, so that the barbs protrude and you can see how long they are. This can be a bit deceptive, especially with saddles, where the barbs in repose tend to lie at a severe angle. A hackle gauge is most helpful for beginners.

On a conventional fly, using a standard hook, the rule of thumb is that the hackle should be 1½ times the gap of the hook. We'll deal with this in subsequent exercises. In the case of the Bivisible, the fly works better with shorter hackle—approximately equal to the gap, or slightly longer. These flies are designed for use in faster, more diffused currents and balance better when they ride lower on the water.

As I mentioned, this fly is composed entirely of hackle. The style used here is known for some obscure reason as **palmered hackle,** which means that it is wrapped over the length of the hook shank, rather than concentrated fore and aft of the

BROWN BIVISIBLE DRESSING	
HOOK:	Fine-wire dry fly, standard shank length, typically sizes 10 to 16.
THREAD:	Fine black or brown, 6/0 or 8/0.
MAIN HACKLE:	Brown, preferably a saddle feather.
FRONT HACKLE:	White, either saddle or cape.

wings, like conventional hackle. As you might suppose, saddle feathers are ideal for this sort of work: They have adequate length and all of the other requisite attributes. We're talking about the main hackle here; the few turns of white at the front can be done with either cape or saddle hackle and can be a bit longer than the main hackle, if you wish. As stated, the main hackle can be whatever color you want. Here, we'll use brown.

TYING STEPS

1. Select a brown hackle and prepare it by stripping off any soft material at the butt end that doesn't have dry-fly characteristics. In other words, strip back to the sweet spot. Leave about ¼ inch (6 mm) of quill for tying in.
2. Tie on a little way to the rear of the eye and wrap neatly and smoothly to the rear. The smoother the thread base, the better the hackle will deploy.
3. Tie in the feather with the front, or more colorful, side of the feather facing you; this will

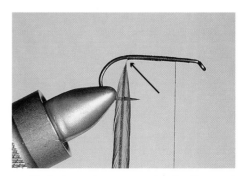

Hackle feather tied in. Note tiny bit of quill exposed (steps 1-4).

The hackle feather being wrapped. Note that the pretty side is in front (step 5).

Tying off the hackle. Note that the thread intercepts the quill (step 6).

The white feather for the front hackle tied in (step 7).

The completed fly (steps 8-9).

result in the colorful side being in front during wrapping, which is very important. Leave a tiny bit of bare quill exposed. This permits the feather to rotate to a position perpendicular to the hook shank, which ensures that no barbs will deploy prematurely and end up slanted rearward at an angle. We want all barbs to protrude at virtually a right angle to the shank.

4. Wrap the thread forward, binding down the quill butt in the process. Be very neat, and cut off any excess quill well short of the eye area. Stop about 25 percent of the shank length before the eye.

5. With a nice, long saddle hackle, you're better off not using hackle pliers; they would only get in the way. Pick up the feather and start wrapping forward, with each turn adjacent to the preceding one. Be sure the colorful side of the feather is in front; otherwise, the barbs will start to lean forward after a few turns. Maintain moderate tension, well short of the breaking point of the quill.

6. When you reach the spot where the thread hangs in wait, hold the feather under tension with your right hand. Pick up the bobbin with your left hand, and execute several lift-over moves, thus binding the quill to the hook. Then switch the bobbin to your right hand and take several more firm wraps. When you are sure the feather is secure, trim off the excess, and lay it aside for future use. Then take a few wraps over the spot where you trimmed, smoothing it out.

7. Prepare a white feather as you did the brown, and tie it in such that the first turn will be contiguous to the last of the brown. Advance the thread forward, but don't crowd the eye.

8. Take a few turns of white, then tie that feather off, as you did the brown.

9. After trimming and securing, make a whip finish.

Hackle Colors

As I mentioned, there are as many Bivisibles as there are hackle colors; more, in fact, because you can mix two colors to form the main hackle. Grizzly works great, as do dark dun and a brown and grizzly mix. Pale colors, such as cream, tend to neutralize the effect of the white front hackle, because there is little contrast.

The major hackle colors are:

Brown Just as it sounds. It can range from a light brown, also called dark ginger, to a rich, chocolate brown, also called Coachman brown.

Ginger A lighter brown, or tan.

Cream As it sounds. It can range from pale to very rich and golden, which is also called straw cream.

Dun This color is somewhat controversial. The Brits have their own definition. Here in America, *dun* is synonymous with *gray*. There are many shades, ranging from very light, which is known as pale watery dun, to almost black, which is known as dark dun. There's slate, which is a rich, dark gray, and medium dun, which is lighter than slate but darker than pale watery. There are also complex duns of many shades that show rust and golden tints. They can be gorgeous.

Black As it sounds.

Grizzly Barred gray or black and white. Also known as barred rock.

Cree Barred with multiple colors. Very rare.

Furnace Brown with a black center stripe. Somewhat rare.

Badger White or cream with a black center stripe. Somewhat scarce in paler shades.

There's a lingering controversy over dyed versus natural colors. It has some historical basis in fact, because until fairly recently, the dye jobs done on hackles were pretty poor, not only from the standpoint of the colors themselves, but also because of what the process did to the feathers.

This is no longer the case. The dye jobs we get today from the top suppliers are excellent, and the colors may, in some respects, be better than the naturals. The only possible exception is with dun: The dyed grays, while very pretty, tend to be flat,

Common hackle colors. Top row, left to right: Coachman brown, fiery brown, light brown or dark ginger, ginger, barred ginger, cream. Bottom row, left to right: grizzly or barred rock, badger, furnace, medium gray dun, pale watery dun, cree.

whereas the naturals often have highlights and overtones. I find these attractive, but I can't tell you how the fish feel about them. In summary—I wouldn't, and in fact don't, hesitate to use dyed hackles.

Some Bivisible Patterns

1. BLACK

Black hackle tied palmer-style, fronted by white.

2. GRIZZLY

Grizzly hackle tied palmer-style, fronted by white.

3. CREE OR BARRED GINGER

Cree or barred ginger hackle tied palmer-style, fronted by white.

4. BROWN/GRIZZLY (ADAMS MIX)

Mixed brown and grizzly hackle tied palmer-style, fronted by white.

5. GRIZZLY/PEACOCK PALMER

A peacock herl body, over which grizzly hackle is tied palmer-style, fronted by white.

Note: These patterns all use the same hook called for in the tying lesson. Please refer to the hook chart in chapter 2 for specifics (page 17).

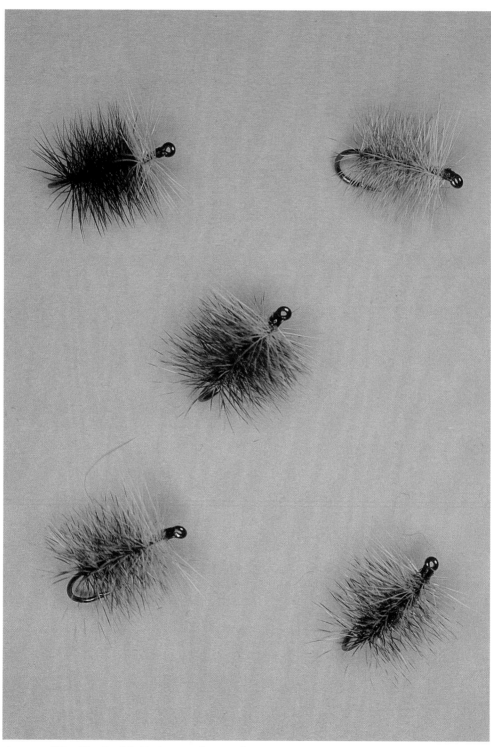

A swarm of Bivisibles. Top left: Black. Top right: Barred Ginger. Center: Adams Mix. Lower left: Grizzly. Lower right: Grizzly/Peacock Palmer.

10

The Hair-Winged Caddis

Continuing to build on the lessons of the Bivisible exercise, let's tie a fly of a design that will enable you to imitate a very important order of insects: the cad-disflies. Entomologists tell us that there are a couple of thousand different caddis in North America, quite a number of which are of importance to the fly fisher. They vary widely in size, color, and behavior.

Many anglers believe that caddis have become more important than mayflies in certain watersheds. This may well be true, as they seem to withstand environmental changes better than the ephemeral mayflies, which must undergo a final metamorphosis into the delicate imago stage before becoming fertile and, thus, capable of reproduction.

A few words about fishing the adult caddis. You'll often see caddisflies popping off the water and fish rising like crazy all around. You are sure that you have a good imitation of the insect, yet you can't seem to entice a single trout. The reason is that certain caddis rise very quickly through the water and take wing directly, sort of like a rocket fired by a submarine. What you see is the rise of fish

If you're at all interested in scientific terminology, the four major orders of aquatic insects the angler has to deal with are identified by the Latin word for wings, which is *ptera*. Caddisflies are of the order Trichoptera, which means "tented wings." Mayflies are of the order Ephemeroptera, which means, in general terms, "ephemeral, delicate, or temporal wings." Stoneflies are of the order Plecoptera, which means "plaited wings." The other major aquatic order is Diptera, which is the largest and includes such beloved insects as the mosquito and the blackfly. Diptera means "two-winged."

nabbing the escaping pupae just under the surface. Often, they aren't quick enough, and a caddis can be seen flying virtually out of the riseform.

A technique that's worked quite well for me under such circumstances is this: Instead of casting above these riseforms in the conventional manner, I smack my fly right into the riseform as quickly as possible. If there's a hungry and frustrated trout lying there, he'll often react immediately, thinking he's getting a second chance at the bug that eluded him a moment earlier. Try this—I think you'll be rewarded. And it's easier than learning how to imitate and present the emerging pupa, which is your other alternative.

The fly we are about to tie is a variation of a great western pattern known as the Troth Caddis. Al Troth immigrated from his native Pennsylvania to the Beaverhead Valley in Montana, in order to pursue the fly-fishing lifestyle. He's now a legend in those parts. The simple but deadly pattern he created to dupe the cautious and selective brown trout of the Beaverhead has become a universal pattern, and we all owe Al a debt of thanks for it.

As I understand it, Al's original dressing didn't have hackle. It relied on elk hair to give it both form and flotation. One of the popular dressings that evolved from this is the simple palmered Hair-Winged Caddis, which has only three components: body, wing, and hackle. This will serve as an introduction to winging the dry fly, which is the part that seems to give the beginner the most trouble.

You probably know already that the caddisfly, when in repose, carries its wings tented over its body in mothlike fashion. This is known in fly-tying parlance as the **down-wing** dry-fly style. It is easier to emulate than the wings of mayflies, which are carried in several positions, depending on whether the fly is in the subadult or adult form. We'll explore that in subsequent chapters.

There are several types of materials you might use for the body. Here, I want to introduce you to a material of fairly recent vintage known as **stretch nylon.** Its most common application is as a substitute for the traditional material called floss (see page 37). Like floss, stretch nylon comes in stranded form, but it possesses some different attributes. It's a tough, durable material that resists fraying during handling and holds its color well when wet. It's a good floater, and thus suitable for dry-fly work. It can be used for almost any size of fly, simply by wrapping layers or using multiple strands. It comes in a wide array of attractive colors. Also, it can, in certain applications, be mounted in a bobbin and used as both thread and body material at once.

Another material you'll meet for the first time here is deer body hair. This is a broad subject, because there are so many varieties of the stuff and a number of ways to use it. Additionally, hair from other animals—elk, caribou, antelope, reindeer—can be substituted for deer hair to obtain certain results. If you get into spun-and-clipped hair tying, which is required for such patterns as the Muddler Minnow, the Irresistible, and hair bass bugs, you'll be exposed to all sorts of hairs.

Depending on the species of animal, and the part of its body from whence the hair is taken, deer hair can range from soft and pulpy to hard and bristly. The soft stuff is what is used for spinning. It flares under thread pressure and can then be trimmed to shape. Very hard hair is used for streamer wings, such as those of the Mickey Finn. It comes from the tail of the deer. Between these two extremes, we have hair that is more manageable, is fairly fine of texture, flares enough to form nice-looking wings, and has good floating properties. That's what this dressing requires.

PALMERED HAIR-WINGED CADDIS DRESSING	
HOOK:	Standard fine-wire dry fly.
THREAD:	6/0 or 8/0, preferably of a fairly light neutral shade, such as tan.
HACKLE:	Grizzly, preferably high-grade saddle.
BODY:	Stretch nylon, green.
WING:	Medium-textured deer body hair, natural color.

Natural caddisflies come in many colors. Various shades of green and olive are quite ubiquitous, so we'll use green stretch nylon here. For the hackle, which is wrapped palmer-style, I favor grizzly, as I believe the barred hackle looks more alive on the water and is suggestive of movement. Caddisflies are nothing if not peripatetic. These short-legged insects ride low on the water, so the hackle is undersized, like that of the Bivisible.

TYING STEPS

1. Size and prepare a hackle per the instructions for the Bivisible (see page 77).
2. Tie on about one-third of the shank length rearward of the eye, wrap to the bend, and tie in the hackle, as you did on the Bivisible. Remember to leave the tiniest bit of bare quill exposed.
3. Wrap neatly to the tie-in point, meanwhile trimming off and binding down the quill butt.
4. Tie in a piece of the stretch nylon about 5 inches (125 mm) in length, and trim off the

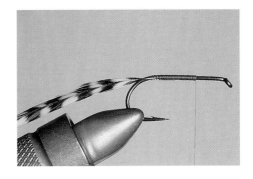

Hackle tied in. Note thread position (steps 1-3).

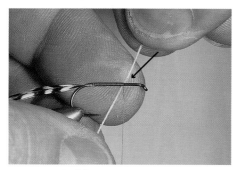

An easy method for tying in materials that have no "backbone" (step 4).

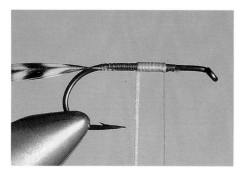

Wrapping the body (steps 5-6).

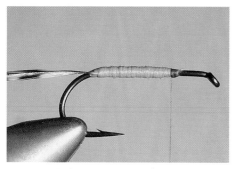

Wrapping the body (steps 5-6).

The body hackle wrapped and secured in place for subsequent use (step 7).

excess. An easy way to control such soft, floppy material when tying it in is to stretch it between the fingers of your two hands, then press it against the backside of the hook while passing the thread over it. This works for yarn, tinsel, or whatever.

5. Wrap the material back to the bend of the hook and forward, forming a double layer. If you wish, you may take one turn of the body material behind the tie-in point of the feather. This helps position the feather for wrapping.

6. Tie off and trim the stretch nylon. Note that these operations take place well to the rear of the hook eye.

7. Palmer-wrap the hackle in spirals over the body, allowing the green to show through between turns. When you reach the front of the body, secure the feather with a few thread wraps, but don't cut anything off; you'll need it to complete the fly.

   Note: If you don't happen to own any long saddle feathers, and are using shorter cape hackles for this fly, you may have to tie off the first feather, make the wing, then tie in a second feather for the front hackle.

8. With the remaining feather hanging out of the way, run the thread back and forth to the eye two or three times, thus laying down a base for the wing.

9. Cut off a small bunch of hair, and clean out all underfur and shorties. As I mentioned in

Tying the wing in place (steps 8-13).

the streamer chapter (see page 62), a fine-toothed comb helps.

10. Even up the tips of the hairs. A stacker is useful here, but if you don't have one, simply remove aberrant hairs with your fingers.

11. Now you have an option. If you wish, you can cut a channel lengthwise out of the hackle on top of the hook. It would look like a wedge of pie from the front. However, this isn't mandatory—you can mount the wing successfully without doing it.

12. Hold the winging bunch in your left hand and establish the length. It should extend to, or just beyond, an imaginary line tangent to the rear of the bend of the hook.

13. Set the wing in place and tie it on adjacent to the front of the body. The recommended method for doing this is to take several soft, or gathering, wraps, then gradually add tighter wraps. This helps keep the hair from flaring all over the place and interfering with what you're doing.

14. When you feel that the wing is secured, trim off the butts, while holding the wing with your left hand, to prevent inadvertent movement. Then, as neatly as possible, bind down the butts, ending up with the thread just rearward of the eye in tie-off position.

15. Pick up the feather and wrap a front hackle. Here, the wraps should be well packed, or adjacent to one another. Tie off and secure the feather, and make a whip finish.

Wing butts trimmed, thread base wrapped to accommodate the front hackle (step 14).

The finished Caddis (step 15).

A little trick: If you have a second bobbin, you can mount the stretch nylon in it and use it for both thread and body material. After tying in the hackle and completing the body, tie off the stretch nylon, substitute the regular tying thread, and proceed with the rest of the fly.

Using these techniques, you can create a host of down-wing flies of whatever sizes and colors you wish. One of my favorites for western waters is the Dark Olive Sedge, the dressing for which follows.

Some Down-Wing
Dry-Fly Patterns

1. BLACK (CHIMARRA) CADDIS

HOOK: Standard dry fly; please refer to the hook chart in chapter 2 for specifics (page 17).

THREAD: Black.

HACKLE: Black or darkly barred grizzly, tied palmer-style over the body, then conventional-style ahead of the wing.

BODY: Black floss, stretch nylon, or fine dubbing.

WING: Black deer hair.

2. DARK OLIVE SEDGE

HOOK: Standard dry fly.

THREAD: Brown or dark olive, 8/0.

HACKLE: Slate gray saddle, tied palmer-style over the body, then conventional-style ahead of the wing.

BODY: Dark olive floss, stretch nylon, or fine dubbing; on very small sizes, just the thread.

WING: Slate-dyed hair.

3. ROYAL TRUDE

HOOK: Long dry fly (2XL), typically sizes 8 to 14.

TAIL: A small bunch of golden pheasant cape tippet fibers.

BODY: Two short sections of peacock herl with a red floss or equivalent belly band in between (like the Royal Wulff; see chapter 12).

WING: A small bunch of white calf tail, tied down-wing-style.

HACKLE: Brown, tied in front of the wing.

4. LIME TRUDE

HOOK: Long dry fly (2XL), typically sizes 8 to 14.

TAIL: A small bunch of golden pheasant cape tippet fibers.

BODY: Lime-colored dubbing.

WING: A small bunch of white calf tail, tied down-wing-style.

HACKLE: Mixed brown and grizzly, similar to the Adams in the following chapter (see page 92), but tied in front of the wing.

A select group of down-wing flies. Top left: Dark Olive Sedge. Top right: Lime Trude. Center: Stimulator. Lower left: Royal Trude. Lower right: Black (Chimarra) Caddis.

5. STIMULATOR

HOOK: Long (2XL, 3X, or 4X) dry fly.

THREAD: Tan or similar.

TAIL: A short bunch of deer body hair, stacked.

HACKLE: High-quality grizzly saddle feather, tied palmer-style over the body and thorax, with the turns closer together ahead of the wing.

BODY: Yellow stretch nylon or fine yarn.

WING: A longer bunch of deer body hair, stacked.

THORAX: Orange dubbing.

11

A Classic Dry Fly— The Adams

WHEN ASKED THAT AGE-OLD ANGLING QUESTION, "If you had to fish dry with only one pattern, what would it be?" I'm willing to bet that most experienced fly fishers would answer, "The Adams, of course!" For while this fly may not look exactly like any one insect, it is very suggestive of insect life in general and has an alluring "bugginess" about it that trout have had trouble resisting for well over half a century.

The Adams is credited to one Len Halliday, a well-known northern Michigan tyer of the earlier part of the 1900s. The original dressing was somewhat different from the one most people tie today. The wings were tied **spent,** meaning that they were set at a flat attitude and lay dead-man's-float on the water; there was also a little yellow ball of dubbing at the rear that represented an egg sac. If I'm correctly informed, the fly was tied without a tail—which figures, because it was supposed to look like an egg-laying caddis, and caddisflies are tailless.

As the fly went through immigration to other parts of the country, especially the Catskills, it was altered to suit the fishing conditions and conventions of each region. The version that seems to have gained favor as the standard is British/Catskill in all respects. It has the four main components—wings, tail, body, and hackle—and the proportions are what we know as **standard,** or traditional.

Even the most standardized patterns of dry fly take various forms: thicker or thinner bodies, longer or shorter wings and tails, more or less hackle, and so forth. Here, we'll tie the textbook style, and you can take it from there to suit your local fishing conditions and preferences.

This fly represents a major step forward in your development as a fly tyer. You'll learn the upright tippet feather wing, the standard dry-fly tail, the dubbed dry-fly body, and the two-feather hackle. This opens up major areas of dry-fly tying, because these components, and the techniques for constructing them, are the very essence of the art.

An observation. In most of the previous tying lessons, you've seen how the execution of procedures early on in the tying of a fly affects subsequent ones. Efficient fly tying is a progressive process of integration. In a sense, it's like shooting pool: What you do now sets up what you do next. This becomes more critical as you move into the delicate and discrete disciplines of dry-fly tying. Being neat and precise when tying on the wings and tail sets up making a neat, well-proportioned body and properly formed hackle. In fact, you'll soon find out that neatness *does* count, big time. It's easier to tie flies with care and precision than quickly and sloppily. Why rush? This isn't a race.

ADAMS DRESSING	
HOOK:	Standard fine-wire dry fly, typically sizes 10 to 18.
THREAD:	Black 6/0 or 8/0.
WINGS:	Grizzly (barred rock) tippets; soft rooster or hen.
TAIL:	Long, stiff hackle barbs; brown or grizzly, or a mix of the two.
BODY:	Gray dubbing, finely packed.
HACKLE:	Brown and grizzly mixed.

A few preparatory notes before we start with the tying. Len Halliday and the tyers of that era used grizzly rooster tippets, meaning small hackle feathers, for the wings. Considering the quality and characteristics of the rooster hackle back then, this was appropriate. With today's materials, many tyers—myself included—favor hen grizzly, which produces a better-looking wing and is very economical.

Initially, I was taught to strip off all materials that weren't to be part of the actual wings. Later, I found that simply folding back the excess stuff nearest the butts worked better, because it provides something to hold onto and helps keep the quills from rotating and skewing the wings. Another plus is that if you miscalculate and make the wings too short, you can easily back off and repeat the folding-back process, whereas once you've stripped off material, it's history. If you prefer to try stripping the quills bare, go ahead, but I think you'll find my method preferable.

The dubbing can be either natural or synthetic, so long as it is very smooth and fine in texture. Personally, I find the new synthetics hard to beat. A brown and grizzly mix is my preference for the tail, but I don't believe the fly suffers a great deal if only one or the other is used, so don't worry about this too much.

As to proportions, the rule of thumb is that the hackle should be 1½ times the gap of the hook in length and should be distributed fairly equally fore and aft of the wings. The wings should be about the length of the hook shank and should be seated about 25 percent of the shank length rearward of the eye. The tails are also approximately the length of the shank, but they can be very slightly longer, if this is required to achieve proper balance. The idea is that the fly should rest on the tips of the tail and hackle, with the hook barely clearing a flat surface.

It is quite important that the tails be spread a little. This not only improves balance, but aids flotation as well. Tails that are tied as a tight clump tend to behave as a wick and draw up water. Tails that are spread or fanned out a bit emulate a snowshoe on the surface of the water, distributing weight over area. You'll see how this is done in the tying sequence.

TYING STEPS

1. Tie on near the eye and wrap a neat thread base on which to mount the wings, using perhaps three layers of thread. End up with the thread hanging about 25 percent of the shank length to the rear of the eye.

2. Select two matching tippets (small hackle feathers) from a grizzly neck, and prepare them as previously described, either folding back (my recommendation) or stripping off all of the fluff and lower barbs that won't be part of the wings. Keep in mind that the wing length is equivalent to the hook shank, meaning from the eye to where the bend begins.

3. Hold the wings with the thumb and forefinger of your left hand with the convex sides against each other, so that they flare apart. Get the tips absolutely even, so that the wings will come out equal in length.

4. Set the wings in position atop the hook at the thread position. Hold them in such a manner as to expose the quills at the point where the thread will intersect them. Keep

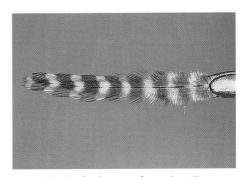

Typical feather for this type of wing (step 2).

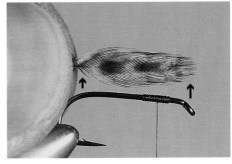

The winging feathers are measured with the hook shank. Note how the barbs are held back to expose the quill precisely at the tie-in point (steps 2-3).

The wings tied on (step 4).

Lock the wings into an upright position and, after trimming the butts, wrap to the bend (steps 5-7).

Lock the wings into an upright position and, after trimming the butts, wrap to the bend (steps 5-7).

A large feather from the edge of a cape, with good tailing barbs (step 9).

them centered. Tie them in place with several pinch wraps, followed by several securing wraps.

5. When the wings are almost, but not quite, locked in, gently stroke them upright. This helps set the wings in perfect position and alignment, because it corrects for any slipping or rolling that went on during the tying-in process.

6. Gently crimp the wings into an upright attitude, then lock them in that position with a few thread wraps tight to the front of the quills.

7. Slope-cut the butts and excess material, then neatly bind it down as you wrap to the rear. This forms a smooth, nicely tapered underlayer and establishes the shape of the finished body.

8. Just at the bend, make a tiny bump with the thread—two or three turns only. This will help spread the tail fibers.

9. For the tail, select a large hackle feather with long, stiff barbs. Complete the barb-gathering procedure per earlier instructions—stroking the barbs to perpendicular, then cutting off or pulling off a bunch. Remember: If the barbs are of equal length on both sides of the quill, you can fold the feather and take from both sides at once. Otherwise, use one side at a time. The tail should be sufficient to support the fly on the water, but not so heavy as to be unsightly. Check the photos for proportions.

10. While keeping the tips as evenly aligned as possible, set the tailing bunch in position, meanwhile gauging the length, as specified.

11. Tie on the tailing bunch with either a couple of pinch wraps or a couple of soft wraps, followed by securing wraps. In the process, jam them against the little thread bump, so that they spread a bit.

12. Trim the tail butts in such a manner that they integrate smoothly with the wing butts, then wrap neatly forward to just short of the

wings and back to the rear. Try to avoid building up any unnecessary bulk immediately behind the wings, because this interferes with the hackling process.

13. Dubbing the typical dry-fly body is a study in minimalism. Tease out the dubbing and spin it on gradually in very tiny amounts. Try to lay the fibers parallel to the thread. If possible, build in a slight taper. As to proportions, if you are working, for example, on a size 12 hook, $1\frac{1}{4}$ to $1\frac{1}{2}$ inches (32 to 38 mm) of dubbing is about right. It's important to end the body short of the wings, so that you won't be winding hackle over dubbing.

14. Wrap the dubbing. The first turn hides the little thread bumps that spread the tails.

15. Prepare two hackles—a brown and a grizzly—per previous instructions. When selecting them, make sure that both are the right size. Either cape or saddle feathers will work fine. In either case, don't cheat. Strip off any material that's not prime.

16. Lay the two feathers together spoon-style, with the brown one in front. Tie them in by the quill butts just behind the wing, underneath the hook, pretty-sides forward, with a tiny bit of quill exposed.

17. Lock in the quills with neat, tight thread wraps, coming forward under the wings. Trim off the quills neatly short of the eye, and neaten up as necessary with some discrete thread wraps. The thread should end up positioned so as to allow for tying off each hackle individually and making a whip finish without crowding the eye.

18. If you're using saddle feathers and they're long enough, you won't need hackle pliers, as you will with the short cape feathers. In either case, start with the feather nearest the front—which should be the brown—and wind forward, each turn abutting the one before. Don't worry about leaving tiny crevices for the next hackle to fit into; the quills will seat themselves.

How to gather barbs neatly for a dry-fly tail (step 9).

Tail tied on, butts neatly buried, thread in position to receive dubbing (steps 10-12).

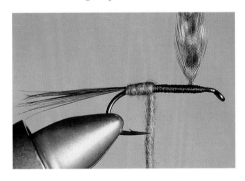

Dubbing the dry-fly body (steps 13-14).

Dubbing the dry-fly body (steps 13-14).

The two hackles tied in. Again, note that a bit of quill is exposed (steps 15-17).

Wrapping the first hackle up to, but not crowding, the rear of the wings (step 18).

19. Depending on just how everything came out, you'll get two or three turns behind the wings. Don't force an extra turn; this would cock the wings forward. Cross over beneath the wings and take the next wrap tight to the front of the wings, which helps support them in an upright position.

20. Take another two or three turns forward—whatever there's room for without crowding—then tie off and trim the feather, as you've been doing.

21. Pick up the second feather and repeat the process. It should integrate neatly with the first one. If you notice any twisting, matting, or whatever, back off and rewrap.

22. Finish wrapping the second hackle, trim, whip-finish, and admire.

Complete wrapping the first hackle in front of the wings, tie it off, and trim neatly before proceeding with the second hackle (steps 19-20).

Wrapping the second hackle completes the fly (steps 21-22).

You've now learned two of the most important types of dry-fly wings. Many patterns call for tippet wings similar to those for the Adams, but using feathers of different colors and markings. There are two things to be avoided: using feathers with too heavy a quill and making the wings too wide. Both will produce skewed wings with too much air resistance. They are guaranteed to turn your leader into a Slinky.

One last note on the Adams tail. As I stated earlier, the dressing accepted as stan-dard today specifies a mix of grizzly and brown for the tail. If you decide you want to tie it this way, here's my easy method for handling and mixing the two colors:

1. Procure a bunch of either color sufficient for half the amount needed for the tail and tie it in place with only two turns of thread.
2. Procure a similar bunch of the other color, take it in your left hand, and hold it just above the first bunch. Match up the tips, so that all barbs are equal in length.
3. While holding both bunches, back off the two thread wraps used to tie in the first bunch. Roll the barbs around between your fingers a bit, mixing them. Then tie them both on together.

Some Classic Dry-Fly Patterns

Note: These patterns all use the same standard dry-fly hook called for in the tying lesson. Please refer to the hook chart in chapter 2 for specifics (page 17).

1. HENDRICKSON

THREAD: Tan or brown.
WINGS: Barred wood duck flank feather, tied as for the hair wing on the Royal Wulff; see chapter 12 (page 103).
TAIL: Medium gray hackles, stiff.
BODY: Dubbing: pale tan, reddish tan, pinkish lavender, depending on region (varies considerably).
HACKLE: Medium gray.

2. QUILL GORDON

THREAD: Tan, gray, or olive.
WINGS: Barred wood duck flank feather, tied as for the hair wing on the Royal Wulff; see chapter 12 (page 103).
TAIL: Medium gray hackles, stiff.
BODY: Light/dark segmented stripped quill from the eye portion of a peacock tail feather.
HACKLE: Medium gray.

A flight of make-believe mayflies. Top left: Quill Gordon. Top right: Gray Fox. Center: Buff Hendrickson. Lower left: Blue-Winged Olive. Lower right: Pale Morning Dun.

3. BLUE-WINGED OLIVE

THREAD: Olive or brown.
WINGS: Gray hen cape hackles, small, tied as was done in the tying lesson.
TAIL: Medium gray hackles, stiff.
BODY: Fine, soft olive dubbing.
HACKLE: Medium gray.

4. GRAY FOX

THREAD: Tan, gray, or pale yellow.
WINGS: Barred teal or mallard flank feather, tied as for the hair wing on the Royal Wulff; see chapter 12 (page 103).
TAIL: Mixed straw cream and grizzly hackles, stiff.
BODY: Cream dubbing.
HACKLE: Mixed straw cream and grizzly.

5. PALE MORNING DUN

THREAD: Pale olive or tan.
WINGS: Pale gray hen cape hackles, small, tied as was done in the tying lesson.
TAIL: Pale watery gray hackles, stiff.
BODY: Fine, soft pale yellowish olive dubbing.
HACKLE: Pale watery gray.

12

The Royal Wulff—
An American Monarch

I'D BE WILLING TO BET THAT ALMOST ALL OF THE fly fishers who answered the question posed at the beginning of the previous chapter with a pattern other than the Adams would opt for the Royal Wulff. There are few flies indeed that have accounted for as many fish and as much excitement as this improbable creation. Its original name was the Hair-Winged Royal Coachman, or just the Hair-Wing Royal. Lee Wulff began tying and fishing his novel flies in 1931, but he didn't name them after himself. Allegedly, Dan Bailey did that.

I became pretty good friends with Lee in his later years, but I never pumped him for information about the hairwings. He did say that the two original dressings that he developed were the White Wulff and the Gray Wulff, as they eventually became known. The great success of these new flies motivated other tyers to dream up Wulffs of their own, and also to fit existing patterns with Wulff-style wings, which is how the Royal came into being. I would guess that there are two dozen Wulffs at this writing, and maybe that's a conservative estimate.

These flies are very American. They were designed for the brawling freestone rivers of the mountainous Northeast and would seldom have produced on the placid chalkstreams of England and Normandy. I say that, and yet every now and then some crazy fish takes exception. My late and much-lamented friend Matt Vinciguerra took his wife Judy (née Darbee) to Silver Creek in Idaho, where the fish can calibrate a leader with the best of them. Judy tied on a huge White Wulff and proceeded to nail a rainbow that weighed as much as any two of the properly behaved trout Matty duped with his 22s and 7X. Her father would have been proud of her.

The only tricky aspect of Wulff tying is doing the wings, but once learned, this becomes pretty easy. As a bonus, the two combined techniques—the X-wrap and figure-8—are the same as for the popular wood duck flank wing that so many terrific patterns use. This opens up a vast array of tying possibilities.

A number of hairs can be used for Wulff wings. Size has quite a lot to do with the choice. Smaller hook sizes, quite logically, require fine hair. Lee's favorite was calf tail, but surprisingly, he also used bucktail. At first glance, bucktail doesn't look like it would work, and some of it won't, at least not very well. For winging, fine-textured hair from small bucktails works best. It yields silhouette without unmanageable bulk, and has enough flexibility to be conformed into wings without an all-out wrestling match. Using a stacker is the key.

Getting back to calf tail: Selection is all-important. Length is not the primary issue; you can leave the really long-haired tail for the salmon flies and streamers. What is important is texture and relative straightness—relative, because no calf tail is really straight. As to texture, some tails are much more wiry than others, and while they may be usable on larger hook sizes, they are not pleasant to work with.

I should mention that calf body hair can be a great Wulff wing material. It's much straighter and a little softer than the tail hair, and a lot more manageable. The only drawback is that it tends to be on the short side. If you can find some that runs about an inch (25 mm), buy it and treasure it.

Lee used to tease me about the style of my Wulff wings; he said I made them too neat. We who write about fly tying and have to look at macro photographs of our creations do have a penchant for cosmetics. Lee liked rough-looking flies, and who would argue the point with him? Not me, for sure, but I still prefer to make them at least somewhat tidy. With calf tail, even the neatest wings are plenty bushy.

Lee and I never did discuss tails. I noticed that he used calf tail for this component also, and, judging from the number of fish he caught, it obviously worked, so we'll use it here. However, I prefer a straighter hair, such as bucktail, moose body, or woodchuck tail. I like to stack these hair bunches, because I feel that the neater the tips, the better the balance. On smaller hook sizes, I prefer feather barbs. I should also mention that I don't worry about the color of the tail very much.

In consideration of the types of currents in which I fish Wulffs, I use somewhat more hackle than with my more delicate and insect-specific dry flies. Either cape or saddle feathers will work, but in my opinion this is where the high-quality saddles really stand out. The barb strength and count, along with the very narrow quills, have revolutionized the way we tie Wulff-style hackles. It is perfectly feasible to dress a medium to large Wulff with a single feather of this type, as the hackle will pack densely. All that's required is that you leave enough space to the rear of and in front of the wings. You can also use two feathers, as you did in the Adams exercise. It's often possible to wrap them both at the same time, but that doesn't always work, and it's not a procedure I would recommend for beginning tyers. If you do want to give it a try, don't use hackle pliers. The feathers have to slip around a little between your fingers, in order to compensate for small but significant differences in circumference. It's like the differential on a car, which enables turning corners.

Before we begin, I want to identify three sources of trouble having to do with the wings; these three are responsible for more heartburn than everything else combined. The first, and worst, is trying to use too much material. The second—and it's related to the first—is not manicuring the winging bunch properly and thoroughly. You must get rid of all the junk and short stuff in the bunch and work with only those hairs that will contribute to the formation of the wings. The third is sizing the wings properly. Please adhere closely to the length-of-shank prescription. Hair wings are heavier than other types, and too long a wing will cause your fly to tip over on its side when it's floating down the stream.

One more comment on that first no-no. If you use too much hair for the wings, it follows that your wing butts will be thicker than need be. This gets you into trouble with the hackle, because besides creating bulk, the wing butts create a nonlinearity. There is no such material ahead of the wings, which means that the hackle has two unequal diameters around which to travel. If it's minimal, you can live with this disparity, but if it's significant, the hackle length will be uneven front and back.

I've mentioned several times how useful a little fine-toothed comb can be, and there is no task in which it is more helpful than in manicuring winging hair. It can be used to clean out the trashy stuff, and to unlock the kinky hairs, so that they can be evened up in a stacker. In fact, the first thing I do when I buy a new calf tail is to thoroughly comb it. You'll be amazed at the difference this makes.

Yes, I believe in stacking Wulff wings. The primary reason—and this is much more important than many tyers realize—is that by evening up the tips, you know exactly how much hair you have. Otherwise, there's liable to be a lot of short stuff hiding within the bunch that will contribute nothing to the wing silhouette, but will create unwanted bulk at the worst possible place, and will cause major tying difficulties.

Despite what's been written elsewhere, calf tail *will* stack—but you'll need a fine-toothed comb and a wide-tubed stacker. Remember: You can stack small bunches with a big stacker, but you can't work on big bunches with a small one. This is true in spades with calf tail, because of its kinky texture, which causes the hairs to billow out and bind inside the tube. Also, you'll need to "unlock" the hairs that are bound together by the natural twists in the material. This is done by combing toward the tip ends a few times.

Okay, you don't yet have a stacker. Be sure to clean out the bunch thoroughly; as I've stated, combing is most helpful. Then even up the tip ends as best you can with your fingers, discarding any wild, unruly hairs. You'll be preparing the tailing bunch in exactly the same manner.

ROYAL WULFF DRESSING

HOOK:	Standard dry fly, typically sizes 8 to 16.
THREAD:	Black 6/0 or 8/0.
WINGS:	White calf tail or substitute, as described.
TAIL:	Same as the wings.
BODY:	Two short sections of peacock herl with a red floss or equivalent belly band in between.
HACKLE:	Brown, preferably of rich, fairly dark coloration.

TYING STEPS

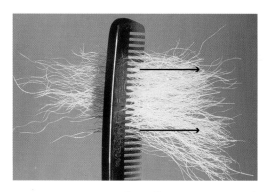

It is very important to clean all extraneous material from the winging bunch. A fine-toothed comb is a great help (step 1).

1. Tie on just rearward of the eye and create a thread base on which to mount the wings, as you did with the Adams, ending up with the thread about 25 percent to the rear of the eye.
2. With the foregoing comments clearly in mind, cut off a small bunch of the hair and go through the various steps to prepare it. Clean out the junk, comb out the tips, and either stack them or even them up manually.
3. Hold the winging bunch in your left hand, tips forward, and gauge length. Then tie it in place on the thread base, using either a series of pinch wraps or a couple of soft gathering wraps, followed by some securing wraps.
4. Before locking the bunch down completely, gently stroke the hairs into an upright position a few times. This ensures that all of the hairs are squarely on top of the hook and

compensates for any effect that torquing action of the thread may have had.

5. Take a few more firm wraps, then cut off the butts on a long slope.

6. When you're sure the hair is locked down and won't slip under pressure, crimp it into standing position with your thumb, thus building in some "memory."

7. While holding the hair upright with your left hand, build a dam of thread against the front. Use only enough thread to position the wing directly upright, and not one wrap more. As you're building this dam, run the thread toward the eye and back now and then, smoothing things out so that you don't create a bump that will interfere with wrapping hackle later on.

8. Now divide the hair into two equal bunches, using a dubbing needle or toothpick. Then take hold of the two bunches with your thumbs and forefingers and spread them, so that they assume a winglike attitude.

9. Now for the first of the two thread operations that form the wings. I call this one the **X-wrap.** Start with the thread just ahead of the wings. Pass it between the wings to the far side of the hook, behind the far wing. Then pass it underneath the hook, come up behind the near wing, and pass it through between the wings again, ending up on the far side of the hook, ahead of the wings. One X-wrap is usually sufficient, but if you need to add another, that's fine.

10. Now for the second thread operation, the **figure-8.** Begin as though you were doing an X-wrap, working the thread between the wings to the far side of the hook, behind the far wing. When the thread is slightly below the plane of the hook shank, take hold of the far wing with your left thumb and forefinger, and, while holding the wing under tension, pass the thread 360 degrees *around the base of the wing*—that is, the hair itself. Bring it

It is also very important to even up the tips of the hair bunch. This is how it is done in a hair stacker (step 2).

The winging bunch tied in and locked into an upright position (steps 3-7).

Top view of the X-wrap, which divides the wings (step 9).

Top views of the figure-8 wraps that shape and position the wings (steps 10-12).

Top views of the figure-8 wraps that shape and position the wings (steps 10-12).

The tail tied on. Note how the butts are slope-cut so that they dovetail with those of the wings and form a smooth base when bound down (steps 14-15).

back between the wings, then down behind the near wing on the near side of the hook, maintaining thread tension at all times. Don't let go of the far wing until you've completed this maneuver and the bobbin is hanging straight down.

11. Now take hold of the near wing and pass the thread *around the base of it,* maintaining thread tension throughout. The thread ends up behind the far wing on the far side of the hook.

12. Repeat the figure-8 at least once, and a third time if it's necessary to form the wings as desired—which is straight up and separated at an angle of between 35 and 45 degrees.

13. Wrap neatly to the bend, covering the wing butts that you slope-cut earlier.

14. Cut a small bunch of hair for the tail and prepare it as you would a winging bunch. Gauge the length: It should be equal to or slightly longer than the hook shank.

15. Tie the tail hair precisely on top of the hook, as you would a winging bunch. After securing it, trim the butts in such a manner that they dovetail with the wing butts. Cover them with thread, wrapping almost to the wings and back to the bend. This results in a smooth, even underbody.

16. Tie in a bunch of four or five peacock fronds by the tips, as you did in the soft-hackle in chapter 5 (see page 36). In the process of securing them, form a thread loop about as long as the fronds themselves. Wrap to the rear, locking in the loop, so that it doesn't matter which end you use. Then cut off one side of the loop and trim the thread to the length of the peacock. Be sure that both the peacock and the thread are collocated at the bend of the hook and that there is no space between the two; otherwise, the thread will come across the peacock and may cut it. If you find it easier to simply tie in another piece of thread instead of doing the loop process, you may do so.

17. Pick up the tag end of thread and start twisting it together with the peacock fronds, in effect forming a virtual chenille. Don't take too many twists at first, because the thread might sever the herl.

18. Wrap the twisted herl and thread around the hook, forming a small ball of herl. Remember: If you run into difficulty with twisting, you can resort to the electronics clip, or regular hackle pliers. Then bind the herl/thread to the hook, creating space for the center portion of the body. The herl is left hanging to the front; it will be used to form the third segment of the body.

19. At the front end of the little thread base you just created, tie in a short piece of red floss or, preferably, stretch nylon. Wrap a little "belly band," working to the rear and forward. Secure it and trim off the excess.

20. Work the thread forward a bit; then pick up the herl/thread, retwist, and make another little ball. Be sure to stay well behind the wings. Then tie off and trim the peacock.

21. As I stated previously, you can use one or two feathers for the hackle. In the case of cape hackles, you'll surely need two. One high-quality saddle feather may yield enough hackle, given its high barb count and narrow quill, but don't hesitate to use two, if necessary.

22. Prepare the hackle feather or feathers per instructions in the three chapters preceding. When selecting them, make sure they are the right size, about $1\frac{1}{2}$ times the gap.

23. I recommend doing the feather tie-in a bit differently with Wulffs than with, for example, the Adams. Tie it (or them) in by the quill butt(s) ahead of, rather than behind, the wing; on top of, rather than beneath, the hook. This allows you to use the quill butt(s) to compensate for and balance out the wing butts. Remember: Pretty-side(s) forward, and leave enough quill exposed so that after you wrap rearward to position the feathers, there will be a tiny bit of quill showing.

The tail tied on. Note how the butts are slope-cut so that they dovetail with those of the wings, and form a smooth base when bound down (steps 14-15).

The first bump of peacock herl wrapped in place, and the thread positioned for the next operation (steps 16-18).

The belly band and second peacock bump completed. Note the space behind the wing and the neat thread base (steps 19-20).

The hackle tied in, as described (steps 21-24).

24. Hold the feather(s) under moderate tension with your left hand. Then lock in the quill(s) with neat, tight thread wraps, working rearward. When you reach the wings, move the feather(s) downward and bind them to the near side of the hook, wrapping back to the front of the body. Then wrap forward again and trim short of the eye. Neaten up and even up as necessary with some discrete thread wraps. The idea is to create as even and flat a base as possible.

25. Wrap the feather(s) per previous instructions, and finish off the fly in the usual manner.

The alternative method for tying in hackle feathers may seem tricky to the beginner, so if you want to revert to the methodology used for the Adams, that's okay. I would recommend that once you become more adept at hackling dry flies, you learn the Wulff method, as it will improve your final product.

Not all hair-winged flies are part of the Wulff pack. However, the winging techniques you've learned here will enable you to tie a wide variety of patterns. Hair-winged dry flies are wonderful in the proper environment. They work great in faster water, and sometimes even in slower currents. They can be used as strike indicators by suspending a nymph or something else below the main fly on a dropper. Once in a while, you might hook two fish at once, one on the dropper and one on the hair-wing. That's always quite a thrill.

The finished Royal Wulff (step 25).

Some Wulff Patterns

Note: These patterns all use the same standard dry-fly hook called for in the tying lesson. Please refer to the hook chart in chapter 2 for specifics (page 17).

1. GRIZZLY WULFF

WINGS: Brown hair: calf tail, or other.
TAIL: Same as wings.
BODY: Yellow floss, yarn, or dubbing.
HACKLE: Brown and grizzly mixed.

2. WHITE WULFF

WINGS: White hair: calf tail, or other.
TAIL: Same as wings.
BODY: Cream dubbing.
HACKLE: Light badger hackle (cream with dark center).

3. GRAY WULFF

WINGS: Brown hair: calf tail, or other.
TAIL: Same as wings.
BODY: Gray muskrat fur or similar dubbing.
HACKLE: Slate gray.

4. BLACK WULFF

WINGS: Dark blackish brown hair: moose body or woodchuck tail.
TAIL: Same as wings.
BODY: Pink floss.
HACKLE: Dark furnace (brown with black center) or dark brown.

5. AUSABLE WULFF

THREAD: Hot orange.
WINGS: White hair: calf tail, or other.
TAIL: Woodchuck tail or brown bucktail.
BODY: Rusty orange dubbing or originally dyed Australian possum.
HACKLE: Brown and grizzly mixed.

While there are a lot of new and innovative materials and methods in the world of fly tying today, I believe you'll find that what we've covered in this book has equipped you with the skills to handle most fly-tying situations and has established a base for progression into more advanced and sophisticated techniques. Best wishes for tying success and enjoyment.

A Wulff pack. Top left: Gray Wulff. Top right: Grizzly Wulff. Center: White Wulff. Lower left: Ausable Wulff. Lower right: Black Wulff.

GLOSSARY OF FLY-TYING TERMS

The following are some commonly encountered fly-tying and fly-fishing terms that supplement those explained in the text of the book.

Abdomen—The main part of the body of an insect.

Barb—The raised-cut section of a hook immediately behind the point.

Barbs—The tines of a feather that constitute hackle.

Bass Bug—A floating or diving bass fly that is tied out of deer hair.

Beard—A small bunch of hackle fibers tied under the hook shank just in back of the head of the fly. Commonly employed on nymphs, wets, and salmon flies.

Blue Dun—One of several commonly used colors in hackling, especially on dry flies. A shade of gray, possibly tinted with ginger.

Body—The main portion of a fly, tied on the hook shank from the tail forward.

Bucktail—A deer tail; also, a streamer fly tied with the hair of a deer tail.

Cheek—A feather tied just behind the head of a fly.

Chenille—A soft, fluffy material used for bodies on wet flies, streamers, and nymphs.

Collar—Wet-fly hackle wrapped 360 degrees around the front of a fly.

Cree—A multicolored chicken feather, having markings of brown, gray, white, and possibly black.

Deer Hair—Body hair from a deer. It's known for its superior floating characteristics, and commonly used for making fly bodies, and sometimes wings. Elk, caribou, and antelope hair are similar.

Dry Fly—A fly designed to float on the water's surface. There are a number of designs.

Dubbing—A procedure by which fur or materials of similar consistency are spun onto a thread to form a fly body; also, the material itself.

Dun—First winged stage of an emergent mayfly; in scientific terms, the subimago.

Dun—Gray, in fly-tying parlance.

Emerger—A type of fly that imitates an emerging insect in the process of hatching into a winged form.

Eye—Used to simulate the eye of a small fish on a streamer fly.

Feather—The epidermal outgrowth covering the wings and body of birds. Feathers commonly used in fly tying include: breast, flank, neck hackle, saddle hackle, herl, crest, pointers or primaries, secondaries, flight, and tippets.

Fibers—Small filaments that make up a feather. The term also refers to other fine components, such as hair.

Floss—A stranded material commonly used in making fly bodies.

Gap, Gape—The space between point and shank of the hook.

Grizzly—Feather from a Plymouth rock or barred rock chicken; gray, white, and black markings.

Hackle—Feathers from the neck or saddle of a chicken; also, the part of a fly that is composed of the above.

Half Hitch—A basic knot used in fly tying to secure the material at intermittent stages.

Hook Bend—The curved or bent section just behind the hook shank.

Hook Eye—The closed loop part of a fly hook to which the leader or tippet is attached.

Hook Shank—The length of hook exclusive of its eye and bend. Generally it's the section to which fly-tying materials are tied.

Hook Size—Determined by the gap (gape) of the hook.

Herl—The fuzzy material found on certain feathers, such as peacock tail.

Larva—The immature underwater stage of an aquatic insect.

Marabou—Soft, flowing feathers, usually from a turkey body, commonly used in tying streamers.

Matuka—Essentially, a type of streamer in which the material along the back is tied down by ribbing material, in order to produce a particular silhouette and action.

Neck—Usually refers to the pelt taken from that part of a chicken; neck feathers are used in fly tying.

Nymph—The subaqueous or immature stage of an aquatic insect; also, the imitation of same.

Palmering—A method of applying hackle over the length of the hook shank or body of a fly.

Popper—A type of surface fly, commonly used for bass and warm-water or saltwater fish. The body is usually made of cork, balsa wood, hair, or a buoyant plastic material.

Pupa—In angling terminology, this term usually refers to the stage between the larva and the adult in the life cycle of a caddisfly or midge; also, the imitation of same.

Quill—The "spine" of a feather; the stem.

Rib, or Ribbing—Spiral-wrapped material over the body of a fly.

Shoulder—Any feather tied to the front of a fly just behind the head, in order to obtain a particular effect.

Stillborn—A term that describes an insect, or its imitation, that is having difficulty emerging in the normal manner.

Spun Deer Hair—Hair applied in such a manner that it flares and spins around the shank of the hook and is then trimmed to a specific shape.

Spinner—The final, or mature adult, stage of a mayfly. The wings are generally transparent or translucent and often lie flat, or spent, when the insect is expiring on the water.

Streamer—A subsurface fly that imitates or suggests small fish or similarly shaped creatures that a predatory fish may strike.

Synthetic Fly-Tying Materials—Fly-tying materials that are man made, rather than obtained from an animal source.

Tag—A component on certain types of flies, located at the rear. Also may refer to the excess, or tag end, of a fly-tying material.

Terrestrial—A land-based insect, or a fly that imitates such an insect.

Thorax—The "chest" area of an insect's body.

Tinsel—Metallic body materials used for the ribbing or bodies of flies.

Tippet—Commonly refers to small feathers from various birds used in fly tying.

Topping—Refers to that component of certain feathers—generally peacock swords or golden pheasant crest feathers—that lies above the wing. Most common on Atlantic salmon flies.

Underbody—The "foundation" of a fly body. Commonly wire for weighting.

Web—The softer, triangular-shaped, shadowy area in the center of a hackle feather.

Whip Finish—A special-purpose knot used for securing the tying thread at the completion of a fly.

Wing Case—That part of an immature aquatic insect (nymph) that houses and protects what will later become the wings. Located on the top of the thorax.

Wings—The term used both in fly tying and in describing natural insects in reference to that component.

INDEX